Rewriting EXTINCTION presents

THE MOST IMPORTANT
COMIC BOOK
ON EARTH

Stories to save
the world

*An anthology dedicated to saving
as many species from extinction
as humanly possible.*

Founder, editor, and art director
Paul Goodenough

EDITORIAL	Will Dennis	**COVER ILLUSTRATION**	Jeff Langevin
	Tyler Jennes		
	Sarah Florence Lord	**CHAPTER ART**	Dan Shearn (Chapters 1, 2)
	Bernardo Brice		Jeff Langevin (Chapter 3)
	Michael Perlman		Jock (Chapter 4)
	Bis Stringer-Horne		Tula Lotay (with thanks)
CHARITY LIAISON	Marie Negus	**INTERVIEWERS**	Paul Goodenough
			Sarah Florence Lord
EXPERT LIAISON	Jamie Woolley		Tyler Jennes
			Bis Stringer-Horne
DESIGNERS	Cornelia Abfalter		Alex Segura
	Antonio Valjean		Maddy Diment
LEAD LETTERER	Bernardo Brice		

Special thanks to:

Hannah Williams, Media Bounty, Climate 2025, Aerian, Ryan Cheetham, Ben Poole, Chris Bingham, Livia Firth, Robert Ferrell,
Dickie Chappell, Veronica Treit, David Baillie, Dan Shearn, Emma Price, Jamie Kelsey, Scott Bryan Wilson, and you.

CONTENTS

DEDICATED TO...

Greenpeace

Fernando Pereira, Photographer (who was killed when the Rainbow Warrior was bombed and sunk in 1985)

Born Free

Pole Pole's death at London Zoo inspired the creation of Born Free. She is symbolic of all wild animals in need, whether free or living in captivity, that we have dedicated our lives to helping.

Rewilding Europe

Rory Young, Conservationist/Wildlife Preservationist

Reserva

Finley Broaddus, Environmental Advocate

Stop Ecocide International

Polly Higgins, lawyer and co-founder

World Land Trust

Dedicated to all the people who are still trying to make a difference.

The Editors

Dedicated to all the species who lost their fight with extinction, and to those fighting for survival right now.

BY
BUYING
THIS BOOK
YOU ARE DIRECTLY
HELPING US CHANGE LAWS
PROTECT SPECIES AND RESTORE
THE DAMAGE DONE TO OUR
PLANET.

BUT NONE OF THIS IS POSSIBLE WITHOUT YOU.
WITHOUT YOUR DEDICATION AND ACTION.

YOU ARE NOT VOICELESS.
YOU ARE NOT POWERLESS.
YOU CAN HELP.

AND IF YOU'D LET US
WE'D LOVE TO SHOW YOU HOW...

FOREWORDS

SCOTT SNYDER

WRITER,
BATMAN, UNDISCOVERED
COUNTRY, NOCTERRA

Comics. What are they? To most people they're books about caped heroes, individuals with extraordinary powers who fight universe-shattering battles. And comics are about these folks, yes, but like their titular superheroes, beneath the tights and masks, comics have a secret identity, a true face. See, deep down, at the most fundamental level, comics are about connection.

Every comic is an act of expression, an attempt to reach across distances—some literal, some existential, all real—to connect with someone else in wonder, in fear, in hope. The very act of creating them is connective. They're collaborative by nature. To make one requires sharing your deepest aspirations and anxieties with all these other people—creative partners, editors…it's a collective creation. And comic books like THIS are hardest of all to make, but also the most rewarding. So many great talents coming together to connect with you about an issue that affects us all—our ecological crisis and the urgent, dire need for ACTION.

So thank you for picking this book up. Because it is a true comic. One that inverts the old formula, maybe, but in the best way: instead of luring you in with aliens and lasers, it shows you what it's about first. Then asks YOU to don the tights, the capes, and go out and be superheroes. To get out there and change it for the better.

PAUL GOODENOUGH

FOUNDER

One day soon, these words will be obsolete...

...people will screw their face up at the idea that at one point in history, which is now, of course, there was once two hundred species going extinct every day.

They'll ask us, "What did you do during the climate crisis? What did you do to help?"

Well, we made this. Three hundred of the most passionate, astounding, and beautiful people on the planet got together and devoted their hearts and lives to making a collection of stories that could save as many species from extinction as humanly possible.

We made this book for every one of you.

We made it to help you help them—the species who have no voice.* We hope our stories open your hearts and your minds and give you the direction and power you need to join us in this fight.

Because if they do, today's problems, and every word I've written, will be obsolete. And we'll all be able to say we helped save the planet.

And what a wonderful thing that will be.

Correct at time of writing. Check out Peter Gabriel's Interspecies Internet if you want to see how him and some amazing people are helping us (quite literally) talk to the animals.

CHAPTER ONE
CHANGE
THE SYSTEM

Humanity is starting to realize that the system we've built cannot go on. We cannot have infinite growth on a finite planet. The following stories highlight some of the current global systems and practices that are sending us spiraling into oblivion.

With the help of organizations like Greenpeace, Stop Ecocide International, along with experts and other charities, our aim with this project is to highlight, challenge, and rewrite the system, forever.

Sponsored project:

GREENPEACE

MAKE EARTH GREAT AGAIN

WRITTEN BY
PAUL GOODENOUGH
ART BY
SERG ACUÑA
LETTERING BY
BERNARDO BRICE

RELATIONSHIPS CAN CHANGE

DEVELOPED WITH	WRITTEN BY	ART & LETTERING BY
TOM MUSTILL	PAUL GOODENOUGH	SARAH GRALEY

It was a normal morning. I'm a composer. It's a job, believe it or not. I'm **meant** to be working on a score...

...but I wasn't doing anything until I had more coffee inside me and did the morning scroll.

My feed did what it promises, what it's designed to do.

I was simultaneously sated and left hungry.

A friend had posted. She lived on the other side of the world.

I did the strangest thing.

I paid attention.

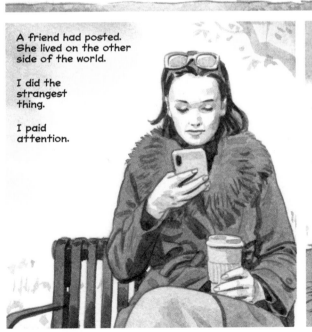

I hadn't seen her for ages. She may as well not exist, really...

Sometimes it's hard to believe we all look up at the same sky.

She shared some lyrics she'd written...

They were heartfelt, lonely, wanting. The light hit the image *just so*. It made me presume she'd used a filter.

But no. It was real.

She said it's an actual song. There's a melody and everything.

She hadn't posted the actual score.

I had no idea how the song goes...

...but she assured us all there is a melody.

I had to use my imagination.

I tried, thinking of distant people, and how we connect and...

Well, using your imagination is an act of seeing.

And, in that moment, I started to see *more*.

And a train of thought provoked by a distant friend, an unheard melody reached an unexpected destination...

I saw notes.

No note played in the same space is alone. They *interact*. That's what melody is.

I thought of the world as melody.

And if there's a connected melody, and the world is an orchestra playing it, it means other things.

Notes can be discordant.

A single note can harm that harmony.

And we can all question what power we truly have... but at the least, you have the power to not play discordant notes.

And encourage others to do likewise.

Because the melody is a beautiful thing, and it'd be a tragedy to lose it.

I decided I'd try to sing in tune with this melody. I'd find the best place for me to play in this orchestra...

That was it.

Nothing dramatic. Nothing super heroic. Just a decision. I decided and I did.

That was
my moment.

Then 7,799,999,999
or so people had
their own.

We each learned
to think of the
world differently.

And when we thought
of it differently, so did
our understanding of
what was possible.

We reimagined societies.
We reimagined ourselves.

We put nature at the
heart of culture and
make happiness the
marker of progress.

Communities came together to
reclaim their agency and create
their own food networks, energy
companies and housing.

No one waited around
for governments to
save the day. We did it,
together.

We imagined. We acted.

And that's how
we saved the
world.

Melody

DEVELOPED WITH
CARA DELEVINGNE
AND ECORESOLUTION
WRITTEN BY
KIERON GILLEN
ART & LETTERING BY
SEAN PHILLIPS

THE BUNKER

DEVELOPED WITH	WRITTEN BY	ART & LETTERING BY
CARA DELEVINGNE AND ECORESOLUTION	PAUL GOODENOUGH & DAMI LEE	DAMI LEE

SMOTHER EARTH

DEVELOPED WITH
JOJO MEHTA

WRITTEN & DRAWN BY
HANNAH HILLAM

DID YOU KNOW THAT IN MOST OF THE WORLD, DESTRUCTION OF NATURE ISN'T A CRIME?

By Jojo Mehta

WHAT DOES THAT MEAN?

Well, most laws about how we treat the natural living world are in the form of environmental regulations, lists of detailed "do's and don'ts." Big companies pay expensive lawyers to work around these rules, and often get little more than a fine and a slap on the wrist if they don't follow them.

What we need to do is make destroying the planet an international crime.

This means the people who make the decisions can't hide behind their businesses, but can be brought to justice individually and held personally responsible.

Chief executives, board members, and key decision makers in the world's most destructive companies could face jail time if their decisions lead directly to serious planetary damage.

Imagine what a difference this would make...

WHY IS IT SO IMPORTANT?

Protecting the future of life on Earth means stopping the mass damage and destruction of ecosystems taking place globally.

We call this serious harm to nature Ecocide. And right now, in most of the world, no-one is held responsible for it.

It's time to change the rules.

It's time to make Ecocide an international crime.

Together with lawyers, diplomats, and civil society, we* work toward amending the Rome Statute of the International Criminal Court to include a crime of Ecocide.

The Rome Statute governs the "most serious crimes of concern to the international community as a whole," currently Genocide, Crimes Against Humanity, War Crimes, and the Crime of Aggression.

By adding Ecocide to this list, we send a powerful message to the whole world that severe harm to nature is both legally and morally unacceptable.

WHAT DOES THAT MEAN?

Follow Stop Ecocide International for more information and actions you can take.

*Stop Ecocide International (global campaign) and the Stop Ecocide Foundation (NL charitable foundation)

ECOCIDE

DEVELOPED WITH — JOJO MEHTA | WRITTEN BY — PAUL GOODENOUGH & HANNAH HILLAM | ART & LETTERING BY — HANNAH HILLAM

THE XR DIARIES

WRITTEN BY
JOHN WAGNER
ART BY
LEONARDO MARCELLO GRASSI
LETTERING BY
BERNARDO BRICE

LIAM NORTON, ELECTRICIAN. U.K.

I HEARD ABOUT EXTINCTION REBELLION FROM THE LETTER IN THE GUARDIAN AND WENT TO THE BRIDGE BLOCKADE, JUST TO SEE WHAT WAS GOING ON REALLY.

IT GOT ME INTERESTED ENOUGH TO ATTEND A "HEADING FOR EXTINCTION" MEETING. UNTIL THEN, I SUPPOSE, I'D BEEN IN DENIAL. OH, I KNEW THERE WAS A PROBLEM WITH THE CLIMATE, I JUST HADN'T REALIZED HOW BAD THINGS WERE. OR PERHAPS I DIDN'T WANT TO KNOW.

I REMEMBER SAYING TO ONE OF THE PEOPLE LEADING THE MEETING--"IF EVERYTHING YOU'VE SAID IS TRUE THEN OUR JOBS DON'T MATTER."

A COUPLE OF WEEKS LATER I WAS THROWING FAKE BLOOD OUTSIDE DOWNING STREET.

"I'd been in denial."

*I SEE GETTING ARRESTED AS A NECESSARY SACRIFICE, ANOTHER WAY OF HELPING TO FORCE CHANGE. BECAUSE THE GREAT MOMENTS IN HISTORY HAVE ONLY COME ABOUT BECAUSE PEOPLE WERE WILLING TO STAND UP FOR WHAT THEY BELIEVED IN. TO **DO** SOMETHING.*

*IF THERE'S ONE THING I'D SAY ABOUT GETTING ARRESTED, IT'S DON'T BE INTIMIDATED BY IT. BEING ARRESTED MEANS YOUR ACTIONS RIPPLE THROUGH THE LEGAL SYSTEM-- WHICH IS EXPENSIVE AND DISRUPTING FOR THEM, AND **FORCES** THEM TO PAY ATTENTION.*

ALSO, AS A WHITE MAN, I'M IN A PRIVILEGED POSITION-- THE SYSTEMATIC INJUSTICES MAKE IT MUCH HARDER FOR PEOPLE OF COLOR TO GET INVOLVED WITH THESE KINDS OF ACTIONS. THE MORE OF US THAT DISRUPT THE SYSTEM, THE MORE THE SYSTEM WILL BE FORCED TO CHANGE.

I'M CONVINCED THE JUDGE WAS SWAYED BY OUR ARGUMENTS, ENOUGH TO FIND A TECHNICALITY TO GIVE US A NOT GUILTY VERDICT. HER OWN KIND OF REBELLION. EVEN PEOPLE AT THE TOP OF THE SYSTEM CAN SEE THE DANGER OUR PLANET IS IN.

SINCE THEN I'VE TAKEN PART IN LOADS MORE ACTIONS. I'M GETTING QUITE USED TO BEING ARRESTED ACTUALLY. ONCE YOU'VE REALIZED WHAT A CATASTROPHE COULD BE COMING OUR WAY, BEING ARRESTED IS NOTHING.

ACT NOW

I VOLUNTEERED TO HELP THE RELIEF MISSION IN LAMU DURING THE TERRIBLE DROUGHT IN 2017. WHAT I SAW BROKE MY HEART.

FAZEELA MUBARAK, ACCOUNTANT. KENYA.

THE RAINS HAD FAILED, AND TEMPERATURES WERE UNUSUALLY HIGH. DESOLATION AND DESPERATION WERE EVERYWHERE, CORPSES OF ANIMALS SCATTERED ON THE GROUND.

"People are right now dying from the effects of climate change."

ANIMALS THAT STILL SURVIVED WERE SEARCHING DESPERATELY FOR WATER. MANY COVERED THEMSELVES IN MUD AS PROTECTION FROM THE SUN. SOME, THAT VENTURED TOO FAR INTO THE MUDHOLE, NEVER ESCAPED.

FOR THOUSANDS OF YEARS THE PEOPLE HAVE LIVED IN HARMONY WITH ANIMALS, BUT IT IS A DELICATE ECOSYSTEM, EASILY UPSET, AND PROLONGED DRY SEASONS CAUSED BY CLIMATE CHANGE PUT IT UNDER A TERRIBLE STRAIN.

PEOPLE WERE SUFFERING, BUT STILL THEY ASKED US TO HELP THE ANIMALS FIRST. ANIMALS DESPERATE FOR FOOD AND WATER CAN TRAMPLE FARMS AND DESTROY VILLAGES.

PEOPLE NEED HELP. THEY NEED HELP DIGGING WATER HOLES, HELP TO PROTECT THEM AGAINST DROUGHT AND FLOOD.

GIVE THEM FRESH WATER AND THEY CAN HELP TO LOOK AFTER THE ANIMALS TOO.

IT IS A START, BUT IT IS NOT THE WHOLE SOLUTION. THEY TELL US THE WORLD IS GOING TO CONTINUE TO GET HOTTER. WILL PEOPLE AND ANIMALS STILL BE ABLE TO SURVIVE IN AFRICA? I PRAY THAT WE WILL.

BUT TO MAKE THAT POSSIBLE WE MUST HAVE FEWER EMPTY PROMISES AND MORE ACTION. AND TIME IS RUNNING OUT.

CATHY EASTBURN,
MUSICIAN.
U.K.

I WAS AWARE THAT PEOPLE WERE CONSUMING TOO MUCH, BUT I HOPED WE'D BE OK AND REIGN OURSELVES IN. YET FOR THE LAST 20 YEARS I'VE HAD THE GROWING FEAR THAT WE WEREN'T GOING IN THE RIGHT DIRECTION.

WHEN THE IPCC* REPORT ON CLIMATE CHANGE CAME OUT IN OCTOBER 2018 IT TERRIFIED ME. TWELVE YEARS, IT SAID--WE HAD JUST **TWELVE YEARS** TO AVERT A CLIMATE CATASTROPHE.

* U.N. INTERGOVERNMENTAL PANEL ON CLIMATE CHANGE.

MY GENERATION KNEW ABOUT THIS STUFF LONG AGO, AND WE ALL PRETENDED IF WE JUST DID THE SMALL THINGS--A BIT OF RECYCLING, LESS FLYING--EVERYTHING WOULD BE ALL RIGHT. BUT IT WASN'T GOING TO BE ALL RIGHT.

I FELT ASHAMED, AND TERRIFIED FOR MY CHILDREN. I REMEMBER HUGGING MY DAUGHTER AND FEELING RESPONSIBLE FOR THIS WHOLE MESS.

"I need to take action for my children. Or else my children won't have a future."

I'M NOT BY NATURE A DISRUPTIVE PERSON, BUT I DIDN'T FEEL I HAD A CHOICE. I COULDN'T JUST STAND BY. WITH OTHERS IN EXTINCTION REBELLION I BEGAN TO TAKE ACTION. NINE OF US GLUED OURSELVES TO HOTEL RAILINGS.

MEANWHILE, LIAM FOX WAS SPEAKING, DISCUSSING GOVERNMENT PLANS TO INCREASE INVESTMENT IN THE INTERNATIONAL OIL INDUSTRY. PEOPLE IN POWER WEREN'T LISTENING. WE HAD TO MAKE THEM LISTEN.

THE DAY WE DEMONSTRATED ABOARD A DLR TRAIN AT CANARY WHARF I'D BEEN SICK WITH FEAR. I'M A MUSICIAN, NOT AN URBAN WARRIOR.

I DON'T RELISH MAKING LIFE DIFFICULT FOR PEOPLE, BUT UNLESS YOU CAUSE SOME DISRUPTION NOBODY NOTICES.

AFTER CANARY WHARF THREE OF US WERE ARRESTED. IN COURT WE WERE REFUSED BAIL AND TAKEN STRAIGHT TO PRISON.

IT WAS QUITE A SHOCK, THOUGH I REALIZE IF WE BREAK THE LAW WE HAVE TO BE PREPARED TO TAKE THE CONSEQUENCES.

IN JAIL I WATCHED THE DEMONSTRATION UNFOLD ON TV. I FELT PROUD AND PLEASED. WE WERE MAKING OUR POINT.

AT OUR TRIAL WE PLEADED THAT OUR ACTIONS WERE TAKEN IN SELF-DEFENSE. WE WERE TRYING TO SAVE OUR LIVES-- AND THE PLANET.

THE JUDGE INSTRUCTED THE JURY THEY HAD TO FIND US GUILTY OR NOT GUILTY BASED ONLY ON THE CIRCUMSTANCES OF THE ARREST, BUT THE JURY CONDUCTED THEIR OWN LITTLE REBELLION. THEY FOUND US GUILTY--'WITH REGRET.'

I'VE BEEN ARRESTED FIVE TIMES NOW, AND COUNTING. TOO MANY PEOPLE ARE STILL BEHAVING AS IF IT'LL BE FINE, AND IT WON'T.

WE ONLY HAVE ONE PLANET, AND I NEED TO PRESERVE IT FOR MY CHILDREN--FOR YOUR CHILDREN--AND FOR THE GENERATIONS TO COME. WE OWE IT TO THEM.

DETECTIVE
SERGEANT
PAUL
STEPHENS.
U.K.

I JOINED THE
METROPOLITAN
POLICE IN 1983
AND RETIRED
IN 2018 WITH
THE RANK OF
DETECTIVE
SERGEANT.

MOST OF MY SERVICE WAS
IN CRIMINAL INVESTIGATION,
INTELLIGENCE, HOMICIDE, HATE
CRIME, RISK MANAGEMENT
AND PREVENTION.

EVA, MY WIFE, IS SWISS. WE'VE SPENT
MANY YEARS TAKING HOLIDAYS IN THE
SWISS MOUNTAINS, AND EACH YEAR WE'VE
NOTICED THE GLACIERS GROWING SMALLER
AND MORE HOLES IN THE ICE APPEARING.
EACH YEAR IT'S BEEN GETTING WORSE.

IT ENCOURAGED ME TO
START RESEARCHING
GLOBAL WARMING.
THERE IS A WEALTH OF
SCIENTIFIC EVIDENCE
OUT THERE.

IT BECAME CLEAR
TO ME THAT
HUMANITY,
OBSESSED WITH
ECONOMIC
GROWTH, COULD
ONLY CONTINUE
BY EXPLOITING
MORE AND MORE
RESOURCES ON A
FINITE PLANET. WE
WERE DOOMED.

EVA AND I RESIGNED
OURSELVES TO THE
FACT THAT HUMANITY DID
NOT HAVE MUCH FUTURE.

"The danger is so great that it threatens the very existence of our species."

IN 2018 I WENT TO AN EXTINCTION
REBELLION EVENT AT OXFORD CIRCUS.
I LISTENED TO SPEAKERS, CHATTED
TO A FEW ACTIVISTS AND FOR THE
FIRST TIME IN TEN YEARS, FELT THAT
HUMANITY COULD POSSIBLY EVOLVE
TO LIVE SUSTAINABLY.

TELL THE TRUTH

AS A RETIRED COP I COULD SEE THAT THESE
OTHERWISE LAW-ABIDING CITIZENS BLOCKING
THE ROAD, PEACEFULLY EDUCATING
PASSERSBY ABOUT THE CLIMATE CRISIS,
PRESENTED A DILEMMA TO POLICE.

PERSONALLY, I HAD COME TO SEE
LITTLE DIFFERENCE BETWEEN
KEEPING THE PUBLIC SAFE WITH
POLICING AND KEEPING THE PUBLIC
SAFE BY RAISING THE ALARM
ABOUT OUR CLIMATE.

IN THE END POLICE DID MOVE IN. THEY ARRESTED OVER 1,100 PEOPLE, SO MY FIRST ROLE WAS GIVING SUPPORT AT COURT. IT WAS HEARTENING TO SEE THE ATTITUDE OF THE JUDICIARY MELT FROM DISMISSIVE IRRITATION TO WHOLE-HEARTED AND EMOTIONALLY ENGAGED SUPPORT.

I THEN SOUGHT OUT POLICE LIAISON AND OFFERED MY HELP. I ATTENDED EVERY ACTION THAT I COULD AND LIAISED WITH POLICE, OFTEN WITH ANOTHER FORMER OFFICER, TO HELP KEEP THINGS AS SAFE AS POSSIBLE AND ENSURE THAT DEMONSTRATORS KNEW THE CONSEQUENCES OF THEIR ACTIONS.

IN THE OCTOBER ACTION, AFTER THE BAND MASSIVE ATTACK HAD ADDRESSED THE CROWD, I WAS DRAGGED ONTO THE PLATFORM. I RECOUNTED A CONVERSATION I HAD HAD WITH POLICE...

A LOT OF POLICE HAVE TOLD ME THAT "WE ARE BEHIND WHY YOU'RE DOING THIS, JUST NOT *HOW* YOU'RE DOING IT. THERE ARE PROPER DEMOCRATIC METHODS."

LOOK AROUND YOU, I TOLD THEM.

THIS IS REAL DEMOCRACY.

I'VE SINCE BEEN INTERVIEWED ON BREAKFAST TELEVISION AND ON LOCAL RADIO. FINE WITH ME. I'LL GO ON DOING WHATEVER I CAN TO HELP.

WHEN THE DANGER IS SO GREAT THAT IT THREATENS THE VERY EXISTENCE OF OUR SPECIES, AS WELL AS EVERY OTHER SPECIES THAT WE LIVE WITH AND DEPEND UPON, I FIND IT INCREDIBLE THAT APPARENTLY INTELLIGENT PEOPLE DO NOT GRASP THE FACT THAT WE HAVE TO CHANGE DRASTICALLY.

WE HAVE TO CHANGE NOW.

THE MOON.
TOMORROW.

MAN ON
THE MOON

"OCEANS OF
DEEPEST
BLUE...

"CREATURES OF
UNTOLD COLOR
AND BEAUTY...

"A WORLD
OVERFLOWING
WITH LIFE.

"WE HAD IT
ALL."

WHEN
CAN WE GO
BACK?

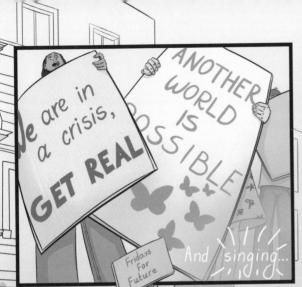

We are in a crisis, GET REAL

ANOTHER WORLD IS POSSIBLE

Fridays For Future

And singing...

ANOTHER WORLD IS POSSIBLE

THERE'S NO PLANET B

... changing the world...

...for us...

SKOLSTREJK FOR KLIMATE

#FridaysForFuture

We cannot eat coal

STORY INSPIRED BY	WRITTEN BY	ART & LETTERING BY
LUISA NEUBAUER AND FRIDAYS FOR FUTURE	PAUL GOODENOUGH	ROSITSA VANGELOVA

Thank you... thank you

Dedicated to the dreamers and believers, from those who can never thank them.

Roots & Shoots
BASED ON A TRUE STORY

MY FATHER USED TO WALK ME TO A PLACE. IT BECAME OUR PLACE. OUR **SACRED** GROVE.

PLACES BECOME MEANINGFUL BECAUSE TIME AND LOVE MAKE THEM SO...

CENTURIES OF LIFE CAN GIVE A PLACE A SPIRITUAL POWER...

THAT MERE MOMENTS CAN'T REMOVE.

HEY! YOU DON'T BELONG HERE.

THIS IS **OUR PLACE.** IT DOESN'T BELONG TO YOU!

LISTEN, PLEASE, THIS IS OUR CAMP NOW. YOU CANNOT BE HERE.

I SAW YOU HERE! AS A BOY! DON'T **PRETEND** YOU **FORGOT!**

WELL?

WEEKS OF LETTER WRITING AND PETITIONING LATER...

PLEASE! WE JUST WANT TO REPLANT THE GROVE. YOU HAVE TO LET US IN.

I CANNOT LET YOU ENTER. CIVILIANS ARE NOT ALLOWED IN A MILITARY CAMP!

YOU SURE ABOUT THAT?!

THEY SAY THEY WON'T BE IN THE WAY.

THEY JUST WANT TO REPLANT THE GROVE AND THEY'LL BE GONE.

THEY'VE GOT PERMISSION...

HMM.

THE CHILDREN... THEY WROTE LETTERS.

OK, FINE.

JUST THE CHILDREN, THEN.

YOU CAN'T SERIOUSLY EXPECT THEM TO--

THE LETTER SAYS THE CHILDREN HAVE BEEN GRANTED RIGHTS TO REPLANT THE GROVE. NOT YOU.

YOU CAN'T DO THIS!

THEY'RE TOO LITTLE! YOU HAVE TO LET US HELP!

THE SUN WAS SO VERY, VERY HOT THAT DAY.

TOO HOT. THE GROUND WAS BAKED...

UNBREAKABLE.

WE'D COME SO FAR... DONE SO MUCH...

OUR FAMILIES URGED US ON WITH ALL THEIR HEARTS.

BUT IN THEIR EYES THEY COULD SEE WHAT WE COULD SEE...

DESPITE ALL OUR EFFORTS. WE JUST WEREN'T STRONG ENOUGH.

IT WAS ALL FOR **NOTHING**. ALL THE LETTERS, ALL THE ORGANIZING...

SO I COLLAPSED...UNDER THAT BAKING SUN, SURROUNDED BY THE REMAINS OF THE GROVE I FOOLISHLY THOUGHT I WOULD SAVE.

OF BOOTS CRUNCHING ON BAKED SOIL AS THEY APPROACHED. BUT I COULDN'T LOOK UP...I COULDN'T FACE WHAT CAME NEXT.

BUT THEN I HEARD SOMETHING, THE SOUND OF METAL BEING PLACED ON THE GROUND...

THE SOLDIERS PUT DOWN THEIR **GUNS,** AND PICKED UP OUR **SHOVELS.**

IN THAT MOMENT, WE ALL FORGOT WHO WE **WERE.**

SOLDIERS...KIDS... FRIENDS...ENEMIES...

...AND WE WORKED **TOGETHER** TO MAKE THINGS BETTER.

AND ALTHOUGH OUR OLD GROVE HAD BEEN DESTROYED, WE MADE A NEW ONE...

TOGETHER.

STORY DEVELOPED WITH
ROOTS & SHOOTS AND JANE GOODALL
WRITTEN BY
CHUCK AUSTEN & PAUL GOODENOUGH
ART & COLORS BY | LETTERING BY
LEE CARTER | JIM CAMPBELL

"LITTLE SUSIE WANTS SOME ICE CREAM.

"SO SHE DOES A *POWER ANALYSIS*: HOW CAN I *GET* THAT ICE CREAM?"

"WELL--SHE THINKS--MOM COULD GIVE IT TO ME, BUT SHE GAVE ME ONE YESTERDAY.

"(AND SHE'S KINDA MAD AT ME ANYWAY.)

"SO SHE GOES FOR *DAD*.

"BUT IF SHE JUST ASKS DAD FOR ICE CREAM, HE'LL SAY, 'GO ASK MOM.'

"SO INSTEAD, SHE HAS TO CREATE AN ATMOSPHERE WHEREBY DAD *WANTS* TO GIVE HER ICE CREAM.

"SO LITTLE SUSIE CRAWLS INTO HIS LAP--

"AND SAYS, 'DADDY! I CRIED MYSELF TO SLEEP LAST NIGHT, BECAUSE YOU FORGOT TO GIVE ME A HUG!

"'CAN I HAVE ICE CREAM?'

"AND SOONER OR LATER... DADDY GIVES HER SOME ICE CREAM."

Dima Litvinov is a Senior Campaigner for Greenpeace, and he explains that's all campaigning really is--

Storytelling.

Dima just *happens* to be telling the most important story in the world.

"THE NORWEGIAN COAST GUARD WAS TRYING TO BOARD US, SO WE SURROUNDED THE SHIP WITH CHICKEN WIRE AND A BANNER SO THEY COULDN'T EASILY GET ON.

"MY JOB WAS TO STAND WITH A BOTTLE OF KETCHUP, AND WHEN THEY TRIED TO STICK A KNIFE THROUGH AND GET IN, I SPIT OUT THE KETCHUP AND YELL--"

AAHHH!

NOOO!

When the Coast Guard finally boarded, threatening to take away Greenpeace's cameras and PR, the ship's Captain replied--

THIS IS NOT ABOUT PR. IT'S ABOUT SAVING THE FUTURE OF THE PLANET!

Words Dima took to heart. Because while an organization trying to change the planet needed that PR, their actions could never be solely about getting attention. Unless it was a **real** protest trying to halt **actual** destruction, it would just be... a bad story.

ARCT

And sometimes it came with a cost.

IN 2013, DIMA AND THE REST OF THE "ARCTIC 30"-- 28 GREENPEACE ACTIVISTS AND TWO JOURNALISTS--SAILED INTO THE RUSSIAN ARCTIC TO PEACEFULLY PROTEST OIL DRILLING.

RUSSIAN AUTHORITIES RESPONDED BY DISPATCHING OFFICERS ARMED WITH GUNS AND KNIVES TO SEIZE THE SHIP.

ACTIVISTS WERE BEATEN AND JAILED FOR TWO MONTHS, SPARKING GLOBAL PROTESTS BEFORE THEY WERE FINALLY GRANTED AMNESTY...

It's one reason I wanted to speak with him. I wanted to know--when the world sometimes seems to only change for the worse, how does he stay motivated?

But listening to him, I'm instead struck by how upbeat he is. His great sense of humor.

And I'm left asking--how does he maintain that?

THE STUFF WE FIGHT AGAINST... SOMETIMES IT'S SO ABSURD. KEEPING SOME DEGREE OF LEVITY ISN'T JUST THE BEST WAY TO DEAL, IT SHOWS OTHERS HOW *SILLY* IT IS.

I MEAN, SCIENTISTS ARE TELLING US WE'RE ALL GONNA DIE IF WE DON'T ACT.

WHY ARE WE TALKING ABOUT ANYTHING *ELSE?* IT'S *RIDICULOUS.*

FACING EXTINCTION'S A BIG DEAL, YOU KNOW?

Someone who's helped get Antarctica off-limits for mineral exploration for 50 years, who's trying to install protections in international waters-- he still believes...

Having a sense of *humor* can change the world. Telling the right **story** can change the world.

So just imagine what's possible...

If we all decided to do just a *little* more?

DEVELOPED WITH
DIMA LITVANOV

Dima's Story

WRITTEN BY
PORNSAK PICHETSHOTE

ART BY
PETER GROSS

COLORS BY
JP BOVE

LETTERING BY
BERNARDO BRICE

Meat Free Monday

STORY INSPIRED BY
PAUL, MARY, AND STELLA MCCARTNEY
AND MEAT FREE MONDAY

WRITTEN AND DRAWN BY
LUNARBABOON

CONSUMED TO DEATH

BY GEORGE MONBIOT
ILLUSTRATION BY IAN STOPFORTH

Consumerism, which we're being told enhances our lives, makes us richer and makes our lives better, actually destroys our peace of mind, self-worth and sense of security.

It constantly creates new needs, new wants, which didn't exist before.

And once we want that thing, our lives feel incomplete until we've obtained it. We forget about what the impact might be on the people of future generations, or on people who live on the other side of the globe.

When we start to monetize our relationships, even with the natural world, everything becomes consumable.

It's not enough to exist as a consumer alone. We desperately need to reconnect with other people and the physical world, the natural world once more. Now is a great time to reassess who we are and where we stand.

To re-evaluate our relationships with each other and the rest of the living world.

To rekindle our moral imaginations, to reconnect and to overthrow consumerism!

Help by pausing for a second:

IS THE OBJECT YOU ARE ABOUT TO BUY SOMETHING THAT YOU REALLY NEED, OR JUST WANT?

HOW MUCH DID THAT COST: MAKE-UP

STORY INSPIRED BY	WRITTEN BY	ART & LETTERING BY
CHEDDAR GORGEOUS	DAVE SCHNEIDER & AMBER WEEDON	WAR AND PEAS

War and Peas

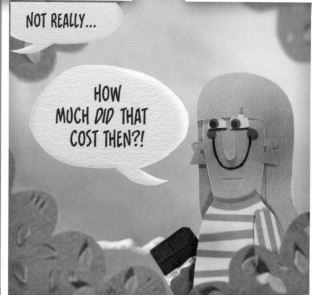

DEVELOPED WITH
PROF. BEN GARROD
WRITTEN BY
PAUL GOODENOUGH
ART BY
DANIELLA ORSINI

Aware Animals   Away

WRITTEN AND DRAWN BY
AWARE ANIMALS

mira petrova

PURCHASING POWER

DEVELOPED WITH	WRITTEN BY	ART & COLORS BY
MICHELLE DESILETS & HELEN BUCKLAND	PAUL GOODENOUGH	HECTOR TRUNNEC

EAT SMART · SAVE THE PLANET · KNOW YOUR FOOD ·

Eat healthy Eat wise

LET'S MAKE THIS LAW

Energy 513kJ 121kcal	Fat 1.4g	Saturates 0.3g	Sugars 8.4g	Salt 0.2g	Enviro Impact 0/5
6%	2%	2%	9%	3%	Unsustainable Palm Oil 0.2g

WRITTEN BY
PAUL GOODENOUGH
POSTER DESIGNED BY
MOKSHA CARAMBIAH

HOW MUCH IS LAND *REALLY* WORTH?

Inspired by Will Travers OBE and Diane Coyle. Written by Paul Goodenough.

You see it across the world—undeveloped land going cheap. Undeveloped, or wild, land is sold at a fraction of the price of land that's already been developed on. What this does is drive businesses and individuals to opt to destroy wild land because they can turn a far greater profit than redeveloping existing, expensive, developed land.

And when they do, the cost to the planet, and us, is devastating.

WHY DOES THIS HAPPEN?

Currently, land purchase price is based upon factors like ease of access, potential for commercialization, restrictions, amenities etc—essentially, how much likely profit can humanity get from the land if they were to transform it into human use, and away from its intrinsic value and ecosystem services it provides in its natural state.

There is almost no consideration to the value the land is already giving. Even to the outputs that directly benefit humanity such as air quality, aiding pollination, carbon sequestration, flood risk reduction, and improving our physical and mental health.

When you add in factors like biodiversity, providing homes to wildlife, maintaining wildlife corridors and habitat interconnectivity, we soon realize the true value of undeveloped and wild land.

We need to change the way land is valued. We need to ensure the planetary value is always factored into every land purchase and the loss to the planet is considered every time land is developed.

If we do this, businesses across the planet would pay more to develop on wild land than they would to redevelop existing land, making regeneration on developed land a more attractive option.

This would not only stop the wholesale destruction of our wild places, but it would also incentivise the re-development of millions of deserted areas like old factories, theme parks and derelict houses – improving our villages, towns, and cities as well.

Join us in calling for this to become law:

> **IF YOU DON'T TRY TO ADD A MONETARY VALUE, YOU'RE PUTTING ZERO IN.**
>
> **AND THAT IS DEFINITELY THE WRONG ANSWER.**
>
> **Diane Coyle** is a professor at the University of Cambridge, leading a project to ascertain the capital value of nature.

COMMERCIAL VALUE

+

ENVIRONMENTAL VALUE

= LAND VALUATION

DYE ANOTHER DAY

WRITTEN BY
LUCY SIEGLE & PAUL GOODENOUGH

ART & LETTERING BY
GOODBADCOMICS

NOT ALL JEANS GO TO HEAVEN

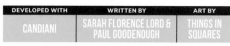

DEVELOPED WITH	WRITTEN BY	ART BY
CANDIANI	SARAH FLORENCE LORD & PAUL GOODENOUGH	THINGS IN SQUARES

3,000 LITERS OF WATER WENT INTO MAKING THESE POLLUTING, HUMAN- AND ANIMAL-POISONING, CARBON RELEASING, MICROPLASTIC-CONTAMINATING STRETCH JEANS, BUT...

I LOOK GORGEOUS!

TIL DEATH DO US PART.

LATER

ONLY THINGS THAT DIE GET INTO HEAVEN. BUMMER, PANTLESS FOR ETERNITY.

SHOULD'VE WORN COMPOSTABLE JEANS

MUCH LATER

PLEASE KILL ME

THINGSINSQUARES

Cruelty What

WRITTEN AND DRAWN BY
WAR AND PEAS

ALL OF THE CREATURES LOVED THE PRINCESS.

WAIT... IS THAT CRUELTY-FREE?

CRUELTY... WHAT?

War and Peas

Fabulous

WRITTEN AND DRAWN BY
WAR AND PEAS

War and Peas

HOW MUCH OF THE EARTH'S SURFACE IS FORESTED?

Since the end of the last great ice
h...

Humanity has been the planet's foremost inventor, hunter, and farmer since we discovered fire, one of our early triumphs we're most proud of.

Of course, being the apex hunter comes with certain responsibilities, which we take seriously.

Consider: mankind is the only species ever to actively save or protect another species.

Some of our most recent highlights include:

THE PEREGINE FALCON! ⊕

With its haughty bearing and beautiful cruel eyes, a top speed of 200 mph makes this king of the skies the fastest animal in the world. Until a human steps into a fighter jet!

THE RHINO! ◯

Although they might look ugly and prehistoric, Rhinos are one of Africa's "big five" and therefore a valuable draw for high-spending tourists.

So rest easy, horny, we've got your back!

THE WHALE! ⊕

Whether they're toothed or baleen, you can't help but be moved by whales' poetic loveliness.

And guess who's doing their damnedest to save them!

Humanity: Annual Report

Yes, we're proud of protecting our fellow tenants of Mother Earth, from the cutest panda to the fiercest cougar.*

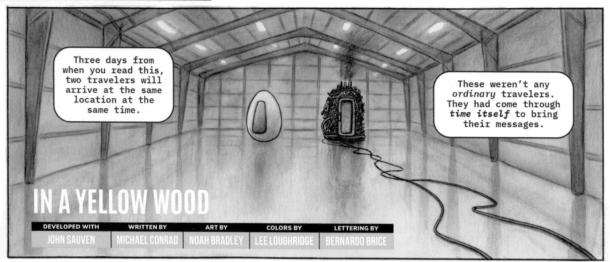

Three days from when you read this, two travelers will arrive at the same location at the same time.

These weren't any *ordinary* travelers. They had come through *time itself* to bring their messages.

IN A YELLOW WOOD

DEVELOPED WITH	WRITTEN BY	ART BY	COLORS BY	LETTERING BY
JOHN SAUVEN	MICHAEL CONRAD	NOAH BRADLEY	LEE LOUGHRIDGE	BERNARDO BRICE

It was unclear at first why they had made the journey. Initial responses were fearful, but they soon made their reasons for visiting clear.

VISSSS

SHUNK
WOOOSSH

Their time was limited; each was eager to share the information they had risked their lives to bring to us.

As we scrambled to set up recording devices, one of the travelers began to speak.

This was *not* good news at all.

PSSSSHH

THE *FIRST* IS SIMPLE: A FOCUS ON FINDING *CLEAN* AND *RENEWABLE* SOURCES OF *ENERGY.*

YOU HAVE THE TECHNOLOGY: A *DIRECT FOCUS* MUST BE GIVEN TO MAKING THESE THE NORM IF WE WISH TO *SURVIVE.*

THE OTHER IS TO MOVE TOWARD A MORE *PLANT-BASED DIET.* ≷COFF≷

THIS MAY *SOUND HARD,* BUT REALLY, IT'S CRUCIAL. INDUSTRIAL MEAT PRODUCTION WAS MUCH MORE *HARMFUL* THAN WE COULD HAVE IMAGINED.

THE LAND REQUIRED ≷COFF≷ THE ENERGY EXPENDED ≷COFF COFF≷ WE WEREN'T SEEING *THE BIG PICTURE*-- THE SUFFERING...

I MUST SIT.

≷COFF≷ GOD, THE AIR HERE IS *INCREDIBLE...*

I TOO COME FROM THE *FUTURE.*

I TOO BRING NEWS OF THE WORLD TO COME.

I COME TO SAY MUCH THE SAME. THIS OTHER TRAVELER IS CORRECT.

THESE TWO STEPS ARE VASTLY IMPORTANT. THERE ARE *OTHERS,* BUT THESE TWO ARE *ESSENTIAL,* THESE ARE THE *FUNDAMENTAL CORE* OF POSITIVE CHANGE.

CLIK!

CLIK!

I BRING HOPE.

HUMANITY WILL DO WHAT'S RIGHT. A RENEWAL OF GREEN PLACES CAN AND WILL OCCUR. A MORE *HARMONIOUS EXISTENCE* WILL HAPPEN.

RESTORATION... OF LAND AND SEA.

WHEN?! ⊱COFF⊰ WHEN WILL THIS HAPPEN? WHAT TIME DO YOU COME FROM?!

HUMANITY WILL *BEGIN* TODAY.

YOU HAVE BEEN HEARD, TRAVELER: HUMANITY NOW KNOWS THE CERTAINTY OF ITS *FATE* IF IT IGNORES YOU.

US.

Y-- YOU'RE ME!

YES. THE WORLD YOU SHALL RETURN TO WILL HAVE BEEN CHANGED. *YOU* WILL HAVE BEEN CHANGED.

"BUT THERE IS MUCH LEFT TO BE DONE. WE CAN COUNT ON THE PEOPLE IN THIS TIME TO DO WHAT'S *RIGHT*."

They didn't have much time left, and neither would we if we didn't heed *their* warning.

Three days from when you read this, two travelers will arrive at the same location at the same time.

We will have *already* begun to *change*.

"Chen *Tai*, I don't normally take a meeting like this but my cousin says you're practically family and it's *urgent*."

"Thank you, Ah Wong. My other supplier fell through and I have some wealthy clients in Shenzhen I can't disappoint."

JUST BUSINESS

STORY INSPIRED BY
STEVE BACKSHALL

WRITTEN BY
AMY CHU

ART & COLORS BY
E.J. SU

LETTERING BY
BERNARDO BRICE

Ah, cops are clamping down. Rhino horn, tiger bone, pangolin scale...

What's next? It's getting so you can't even enjoy a bowl of shark's fin soup anymore.

Traditional Chinese medicine has been around for 5,000 years. Westerners say there's no proof it works. Who needs proof when you have thousands of years of fine tuning?

Belief is a powerful thing. I have a client who has cancer. Who knows? People who have money will pay anything. Personally, if I'm that sick I go to a Western hospital. But Chinese medicine. Just in case.

My wife is superstitious. Me, I'm practical.

S'why I'm Buddhist *and* Christian. Just in case.

So about that rhino horn...?

Listen, you seem like a nice lady. Rhino horn is very, very expensive. And *very* illegal. The going rate is over $60k per kilo.

So much?

Supply and demand. It's just *business.* When there was still rhino and tiger in *China,* they were still expensive. It was never for the peasants.

You have *cash.* I have lots of other things. Come inside. I give you a good deal.

What's he messing with that snake for? @#$%¢ crazy Westerners. Guys like that are bad for business.

Hypocrites. They use feng shui and acupuncture but don't believe in Chinese medicine?

These gwei lo think chicken soup cures a cold.

Yet everyone knows it's the chicken *and* the ginseng.

Do you have any tiger bone?

Heh, right here. I'm a tiger! *At least,* that's what my wife tells me.

What about this? *Real?*

Of course not. You think I'd have a real rhino cup out like that?

Ming Dynasty. Our ancestors killed them all off to make trophies like these.

Just like the Americans and their bison, the Europeans and their dodo birds.

Look, I'm not here for souvenirs or a history lesson. You don't have what I need. I will find someone else.

Okay, okay, here, here let me show you something.

IS FAST FASHION MAKING US SICK?

Every time we wash 5 kilograms of synthetic clothes, 9 million micro- and nanofibers are released into our streams and oceans and end up in the fish we eat. The fibers from the clothes we wear are released into the very air in our homes. We breathe them in, all day...every day.

Scientific research links nylon and polyester fibers with reduced lung cell growth. Just how much damage they're doing is only now being uncovered. And the industry is terrified the truth will come out...

And that truth is: the fast fashion industry has a range of solutions. But they would rather make more profits than use them — and that's why you, me, and the rest of the world are inhaling their fibers.

Demand fast fashion stops trading our health for their profits.

Fashion should be safe for us all.
#sickfashion #makefashionsafe

DEVELOPED WITH
THE PLASTIC SOUP FOUNDATION
POSTER DESIGNED BY
MOKSHA CARAMBIAH

I'M GUY BYRNE-WOODS, CEO OF THE FORESTRY FELLING SYNDICATE.

TIK... TOK...

GUY BYRNE-WOODS FFS

ON BEHALF OF THE GLOBAL LOGGING INDUSTRY, I WANT TO THANK PEOPLE LIKE YOU FOR COLLECTIVELY INVESTING HUNDREDS OF MILLIONS WITH US.

TIK... TOK...

OUR PENSION FUNDS, NO MATTER HOW PIDDLY, ALL ADD UP.

TIK... TOK...

AND WITH ALL YOUR CASH...

TIK... TOK...

TIK... TOK...

... WE'VE BEEN ABLE TO DESTROY MORE NATURAL HABITAT THAN WE *EVER* THOUGHT POSSIBLE.

FROM ALASKA TO THE AMAZON...

TIK... TOK...

...FROM SIBERIA TO SUDAN.

TIK... TOK...

TIK... TOK...

TIK... TOK...

SYNERGY.

TIK... TOK...

WE'VE ALSO USED YOUR INVESTMENTS TO FIGHT PESKY GOVERNMENT RESTRICTIONS.

IN FACT, EVERY SINGLE MINUTE, WE MANAGE TO CLEAR ABOUT 30 FOOTBALL FIELDS OF FOREST.

TIK... TOK...

TIK... TOK...

TIK... BONG

THERE GOES ANOTHER ONE!

TIK... TOK...

BUT WE CAN ONLY KEEP UP OUR RECORD-BREAKING WORK WITH YOUR HELP.

WITH YOUR CONTINUED INVESTMENT WE CAN DO EVEN MORE TOGETHER NEXT YEAR--

TIK... TOK...

TO MAKE MONEY, AND DESTROY THE PLANET.

TIK... TOK...

SO REMEMBER, YOUR MONEY, IS LITERALLY CHANGING THE WORLD.

DO YOU KNOW WHAT YOUR MONEY IS FUNDING?

WRITTEN BY	ART BY	COLORS BY	LETTERING BY
LUCKY GENERALS	DOUG BRAITHWAITE	SEBASTIAN CHENG	BERNARDO BRICE

PENSION POWER!

BY MAKE MY MONEY MATTER

The choice on where to keep, save, and invest your money is more powerful than you think.

In fact, deciding the pension we hold is one of the most powerful things we can do to cut our carbon, tackle the climate crisis, and give our money a chance to grow in the long run.

HOW'S THAT?

In the UK alone, there's **£3 trillion** held in pensions, and it's money that many of us have the ability to control.

But while investing in many vital businesses, pension funds have also been funding some of the nastiest stuff on the planet.

From tobacco to fossil fuels, weaponry to deforestation, pension funds have invested trillions on our behalf without ever asking us the crucial question:

Do these investments create a world we actually want to live in?

This means our money may be contradicting our lifestyles, with climate campaigners invested in coal, vegans invested in factory farming, and scientists invested in tobacco.

MAKE YOUR MONEY MATTER!

But it doesn't have to be this way.

You can make your money matter, and ensure the trillions of pounds invested on our behalf builds a better world.

After all, what's the point in saving for retirement in a world on fire?

Find out more at www.makemymoneymatter.co.uk

MMM

MakeMyMoneyMatter.co.uk

WHILE YOU SLEEP

DEVELOPED WITH RICHARD CURTIS AND VICTOR SOLÍS　**WRITTEN BY** PAUL GOODENOUGH　**ART BY** ABHIJEET KINI

MEET JESS. JESS CARES DEEPLY ABOUT THE PLANET.

I SHOP RESPONSIBLY!

IN FACT. SHE THINKS ABOUT PRETTY MUCH NOTHING ELSE!

I ADOPT, NEVER SHOP!

SAVE THE PLANET

BUT SECRETLY, WHILE THE LOVELY JESS SLEEPS, HER MONEY GETS TO WORK...

DESTROYING MORE OF THE PLANET THAN ALL HER GOOD WORK COMBINED!

PENSIONS BANKS INVESTMENTS

IS *YOUR* MONEY BEING USED TO FUND PLANETARY DESTRUCTION? FIND OUT AT *WWW.SWITCHIT.MONEY*

WE SHOULD WAKE UP RUSSELL.

I'M ALREADY WOKE, MA!

DID YOU KNOW YOUR PENSIONS ARE BEING INVESTED IN ARMS DEALS AND TOBACCO?

WHEN I WAS YOUR AGE, WE CERTAINLY DIDN'T HAVE A FANCY HOUSE WITH INTERNET TO GOOGLE SUCH THINGS.

AND WHEN I'M YOUR AGE, NO ONE WILL HAVE A FANCY ANYTHING, BECAUSE YOU IDIOTS DESTROYED THE PLANET!

I TOLD YOU THIS GRETA GIRL IS A BAD INFLUENCE.

DEAR, HE DOES HAVE A POINT.

HONEY, YOUR FATHER AND I CARE ABOUT THESE ISSUES.

JUST NOT ENOUGH TO CHANGE ANYTHING.

NOW, OFF TO SCHOOL, SON.

SLURRP

Woke

War and Peas

DEVELOPED WITH **RICHARD CURTIS** WRITTEN AND DRAWN BY **WAR AND PEAS**

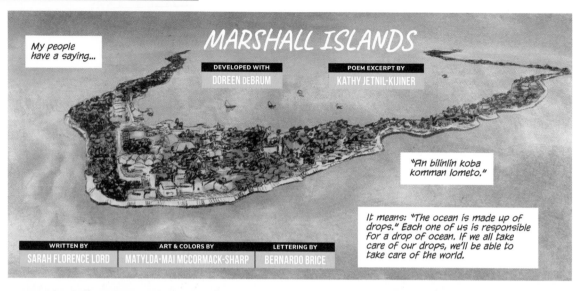

MARSHALL ISLANDS

My people have a saying...

DEVELOPED WITH
DOREEN DeBRUM

POEM EXCERPT BY
KATHY JETNIL-KIJINER

"An bilinlin koba komman lometo."

It means: "The ocean is made up of drops." Each one of us is responsible for a drop of ocean. If we all take care of our drops, we'll be able to take care of the world.

WRITTEN BY
SARAH FLORENCE LORD

ART & COLORS BY
MATYLDA-MAI MCCORMACK-SHARP

LETTERING BY
BERNARDO BRICE

In 2019, I left my homeland of the Marshall Islands to become the UN ambassador in Geneva, to bring the issues faced by my people to the global stage.

If you don't know already, the Marshall Islands is in immediate threat from rising sea levels. If we don't do something, our islands... My home... Will be underwater, and we will all be homeless.

The committee decided it would be me who should go to Geneva and set up the mission.

It was only meant to take six months...

I barely had time to say goodbye to my family...

I was suddenly starting a new life in a foreign country... 14,000 km from home with no money, no transportation and no accommodation.

It was a... difficult... first few months.

When I arrived I immediately began campaigning for us to become a member of the Human Rights Council.

I really struggled to see how I could make people understand how serious the threat to our islands is, how I could make them relate to the issues that my people face.

But I was determined.

All of our islands will be underwater within 60 years. We've already lost one, we simply cannot wait any longer to take action...

If my people become climate refugees what does that mean? Where do we go? As a nation, what do we **become?**

I left my homeland so that my people would not be forced to.

Without our islands we are nothing.

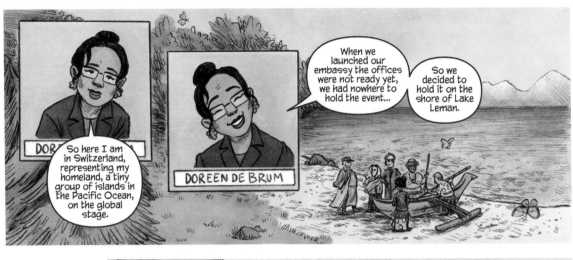

DOREEN DE BRUM

So here I am in Switzerland, representing my homeland, a tiny group of islands in the Pacific Ocean, on the global stage.

When we launched our embassy the offices were not ready yet, we had nowhere to hold the event...

So we decided to hold it on the shore of Lake Leman.

And we had a Korkor, a traditional Marshallese canoe, brought from the Pacific Ocean to the Swiss Alps. It was a beautiful, poignant reminder that no matter where we live, climate change affects us all.

And I was reminded of the expression, "with climate change, we are not all in the same boat, but sooner or later we all must weather the same storm."

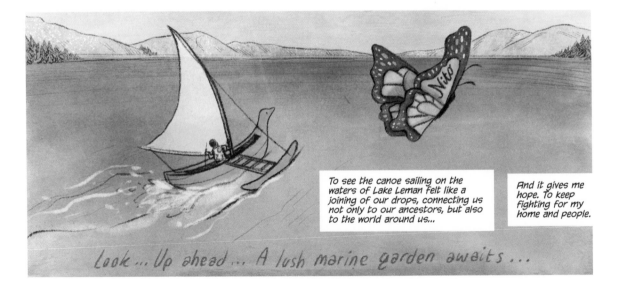

To see the canoe sailing on the waters of Lake Leman felt like a joining of our drops, connecting us not only to our ancestors, but also to the world around us...

And it gives me hope. To keep fighting for my home and people.

look ... Up ahead ... A lush marine garden awaits ...

TED TALKS

STORY INSPIRED BY	WRITTEN BY	ART & LETTERING BY	WITH THANKS TO
PETER GABRIEL AND THE INTERSPECIES INTERNET	PAUL GOODENOUGH	SARAH GRALEY	TED

STEPHEN HAWKING OBSERVED THAT MANKIND LEARNING TO TALK WAS THE BIGGEST LEAP IN EVOLUTION.

IMAGINE HOW THE WORLD WOULD CHANGE IF *EVERYONE* COULD COMMUNICATE, FROM THE SMALLEST INSECT TO THE LARGEST MAMMAL.

THE *EMPATHY* WE WOULD GAIN. THE *UNDERSTANDING*...

WHY...

...IT MIGHT EVEN BE ENOUGH TO SAVE US FROM EXTINCTION.

GASP! GASP!

"I'VE BEEN WALKING FOR ABOUT 30 YEARS WITH OUR INDIGENOUS ELDERS--COMING TO INSTRUCT US, HELPING US REMEMBER HOW TO WALK IN THE ORIGINAL WAY OF LIFE AND TO FOLLOW THE PROTOCOLS OF THE EARTH HERSELF.

"IT IS TIME FOR US TO GALVANIZE AND COLLABORATE WITH INDUSTRIES, PHILANTHROPISTS, GOVERNMENTS, AND ORIGINAL PEOPLE TO FOLLOW THESE INSTRUCTIONS.

"WHAT WE WANT IS TO BRING BACK CONSCIOUSNESS. EVERY CULTURE HAS AN ACTIVE OBLIGATION TO COME TOGETHER TO SOLVE THIS CRISIS.

"TO BRING ABOUT CHANGE IN OUR ENVIRONMENT AND OUR SOCIETY. REMEMBER THAT IT IS THE COMMUNITIES CLOSEST TO MOTHER EARTH AND NATURE THAT ARE THE ONES MOST AFFECTED.

"A TABLE HAS BEEN SET, AND WE'RE ALL BRINGING THESE THREADS THAT MOTHER EARTH HERSELF HAS CULTIVATED.

"THERE ARE UNBROKEN THREADS THAT HAVE BEEN BROUGHT FROM THE ORIGINAL DAYS THROUGH OUR INDIGENOUS RELATIVES THAT WILL GUIDE THE WEAVING PROCESS, SO WE CAN BEGIN TO SEE THE NEW TAPESTRY OF WHAT WE'VE COME TO SERVE.

DEVELOPED WITH
JYOTI MA AND MINDAHI BASTIDA
ADAPTED BY
SARAH FLORENCE LORD & TYLER JENNES
ART & COLORS BY   LETTERING BY
ZOE THOROGOOD   BERNARDO BRICE

"THERE ARE MANY PROPHECIES THAT HAVE BEEN PASSED THROUGH ORIGINAL PEOPLE'S LINES AND THEY HAVE PREPARED US FOR THE TIME WE'RE STANDING IN NOW.

"THOSE PROPHECIES ARE NOW INSTRUCTING US HOW TO WALK THROUGH THIS. MOTHER EARTH IS LITERALLY SPEAKING TO US IF WE JUST LISTEN.

"ACCORDING TO OUR LORE, THIS IS THE EARTH'S SIXTH EXTINCTION. SHE KNOWS HOW TO HANDLE IT IF WE JUST LET HER.

"SHE HAS SENT HER ORIGINAL PEOPLE TO HELP US THROUGH THESE TIMES, AND WE MUST RADICALLY LISTEN TO HER INSTRUCTION.

"WHEN YOU SEE A RAINBOW, YOU SEE THE COLORS. IF ONE COLOR IS MISSING, IT IS NO LONGER A RAINBOW."

THERE IS A SAYING IN OUR CULTURE...

LESSONS FROM THE LAKOTA

DEVELOPED WITH
MOSES BRINGS PLENTY
WRITTEN BY
SARAH FLORENCE LORD
ART & COLORS BY
ZOE THOROGOOD
LETTERING BY
BERNARDO BRICE

"LÉ WANJI PHEŽÍ OTHÓKAHE MAKHÁ WIČHÓNI."

IT MEANS: THIS ONE GRASS IS THE BEGINNING OF LIFE ON EARTH.

IF THE GRASS IS HEALTHY THEN THE BISON ARE HEALTHY. IF THE BISON ARE HEALTHY THEN WE ARE ALL HEALTHY. THIS IS THE SACRED CIRCLE OF LIFE THAT MUST NOT BE INTERRUPTED.

THE ROOTS OF THE GRASS SHOULD BE SIX FEET DEEP.

BUT THEY HAVE RETREATED. THEY ARE DAMAGED BY ALL THE CHEMICALS WE SPRAY, THE MACHINERY WE USE, THE METHODS WE APPLY.

THE EARTH IS WOUNDED. SHE HAS OPEN SCARS.

BUT LIKE A SCAB WE KEEP PICKING AT THEM...

THE EARTH IS OUR SHARED BODY.

THE RAINFORESTS ARE OUR LUNGS--

--THE CORAL REEFS OUR ARTERIES--

--SO WHY DO WE CONTINUE TO POISON OURSELVES?

FOR SOME REASON WE BELIEVE THAT THE EARTH NEEDS US TO DO HER JOB FOR HER, A JOB THAT SHE HAS ALREADY BEEN DOING FOR CENTURIES.

THE BUFFALO, WITH HIS SPLIT HOOVES, TILLS THE EARTH...

...AND THE HORSE SOWS THE SEEDS, USING HIS TAIL TO BRUSH THEM FROM THE CROPS AND HIS FLAT HOOVES TO PLANT THEM INTO THE EARTH.

THE BUFFALO AND THE HORSE PERFORM THEIR RITUALS TO RESTORE THE EARTH. I'VE SEEN THE BUFFALO DANCE ACROSS THE PLAIN, JUMPING INTO THE AIR LIKE DEER!

THE VIBRATION OF THEIR MOVEMENTS SPEAKS TO THE SOIL. IT TELLS IT IS SAFE TO BE WILD AGAIN.

THE HORSE FOLLOWS THE SAME PATH AS THE BUFFALO. IT IS JUST LIKE A DANCE. THEY DO THE CEREMONY TWO, THREE TIMES EACH...

...AND THE FINAL TIME THEY DO IT TOGETHER.

THE SPIRIT OF THE EARTH IS COMING BACK BECAUSE WE HAVE **GIVEN** IT BACK. THE EARTH KNOWS MORE THAN US. SHE WILL HEAL HERSELF IF WE GIVE HER A CHANCE.

IT IS MY HOPE THAT ONE DAY WE WILL LEARN TO STOP THINKING OF THE EARTH AS OUR RESOURCE, AND INSTEAD AS THE SOURCE TO OUR LIVES, ALL LIFE.

EVERYTHING HAS BEEN GIVEN TO US; IT DOESN'T MEAN WE HAVE TO TAKE IT.

YOU UNDERSTAND, T'UNSHKÁ?

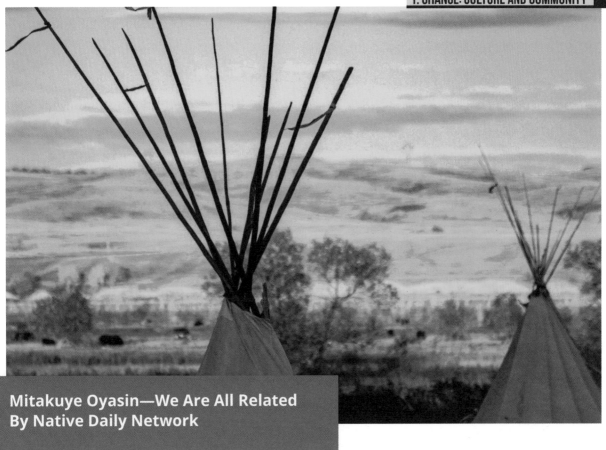

Mitakuye Oyasin—We Are All Related
By Native Daily Network

Traditional Indigenous teachings are an important connection to a time before paradise was lost in all but a few corners of the planet.

CONNECTIONS RUN DEEP.

The Lakota have a saying for this; Mitakuye Oyasin. Roughly translated, it means 'We Are All Related.'

It is an affirmation of a very real connection that exists between all things.

Our interconnected existence is celebrated and cherished. It is a way of life that places us as part of the natural world, not apart from it.

It means that everything is our relative, from the smallest amoeba to the largest whale. From the forests to the water flowing through our rivers. In this way of life, it is understood that each relative has their own, equally important part to play in the natural order.

As Water Protectors we are part of a global community of people that are standing up to protect Unci Maka—Grandmother Earth.

When people ask the Lakota why they fight so hard to protect their waters, they say 'Mni Wiconi'—Water of Life.

WITHOUT IT, THERE IS NO LIFE.
WITHOUT THAT, THERE IS NO US.

MBAGATHI HIGH SCHOOL, 15 KM OUTSIDE NAIROBI CITY.

NO TREES, NO FLOWERS, NO GRASS FOR THEM TO SIT ON.

YOU SEE WHAT I'M SAYING?

HOW CAN WE EXPECT THIS GENERATION TO HAVE ANY CONNECTION TO THEIR ENVIRONMENT?

GREENING SCHOOLS

EVERYONE NEEDS TO BE PART OF THE SOLUTION. YOU. ME. THESE KIDS.

AND IT STARTS HERE.

TEN YEARS LATER.

NO NEW FOSSIL FUEL

NO MORE EXCAVATION NO! NO!

STOP!

YEAH, YEAH, I KNOW...

BUT THE COURT RULED IN OUR FAVOR...AND OUR ORDERS ARE TO CARRY ON WITH THIS JOB!

--WITNESSED THE INCREDIBLE RESULTS OF OUR INVESTMENT STRATEGIES IN KENYA. IT MAKES US ALL FEEL GOOD TO KNOW WE'VE MADE A DIFFERENCE.

AND NOW...DO ANY OF YOU KIDS HAVE QUESTIONS?

I HAVE A QUESTION...DO YOU THINK IT'S FAIR THAT AFRICA ONLY CONTRIBUTES AROUND 5% OF GLOBAL GREENHOUSE GAS EMISSIONS...

BUT SUFFERS A FAR GREATER PROPORTION OF THE RESULTING CLIMATE CHANGE IMPACT?

BENEATH THE TREES

DEVELOPED WITH	WRITTEN BY	ART & LETTERING BY
ELIZABETH WATHUTI	DAVID BAILLIE	JUNI BA

THIS IS SUPPOSED TO BE A SOFTBALL Q&A WITH A CROWD OF PHOTOGENIC KIDS. WHAT'S GOING ON?

OK, LET'S GET SOME MORE QUESTIONS.

YOU, YOU THERE WITH YOUR HAND UP. WHAT DO YOU WANT TO ASK THE PRESIDE--

THANKS.

MY QUESTION CONCERNS THE RECENTLY REJECTED PLANS FOR CARBON SINKS IN NAIROBI.

AIR POLLUTION IS A LEADING CAUSE IN THE CURRENT PUBLIC HEALTH CRISIS. AND THOSE CARBON SINKS WOULD HAVE HELPED REDUCE--

WHAT? WHY-- I MEAN.

BARRY, WHERE DID YOU FIND BLOODY RADICALIZED KIDS? I WANT TO KNOW WHO THE HELL HIJACKED MY CAREFULLY PLANNED PR VICTORY LAP HERE? HUH?!

YOU SHOULD NOT HOLD THESE EVENTS IN ORDER TO FEEL BETTER ABOUT YOURSELVES.

PARDON ME?

IF SOMEONE SAYS SOMETHING YOU DO NOT LIKE HERE, THEN YOU SHOULD INVESTIGATE THE CLAIM, NOT THE PERSON WHO SAID IT.

JUST TELL ME, BARRY. WHO ARE THESE KIDS? WHAT ARE THEIR NAMES? THESE...TROUBLE MAKERS.

WHAT ARE THEIR NAMES?

-KZZRT-

THESE TROUBLE MAKERS.

"I FIND MOMENTS OF PEACE IN OUR FRONT YARD. IT'S WHERE MY PLANTS ARE AND WHERE I GO EVERY MORNING AND AFTERNOON. I FEEL AT PEACE KNOWING THAT PEOPLE WHO TRUSTED ME THEN STILL HAVE CONFIDENCE IN ME AND CONTINUE TO SUPPORT ME NOW.

"BEFORE, MY SOURCE OF MOTIVATION WERE MY PARENTS, BUT BOTH OF THEM PASSED AWAY LAST YEAR. THEY WERE MY INSPIRATION. NOW, I ENJOY THE COMPANY OF MY NEPHEWS AND NIECES WHO ARE ALWAYS HERE.

"OF COURSE, I AM HOPEFUL THE GLOBAL COMMUNITY CAN CHANGE THEIR ATTITUDES TOWARD CLIMATE CHANGE.

"FOR ME, WE SHOULD NOT BE DRIVEN BY PRIDE OR EGO. WE SHOULD BE DANCING TO THE SAME BEAT. IF WE WANT TO ADDRESS THE PROBLEM OF CLIMATE CHANGE, GLOBALLY WE MUST BE UNITED. BECAUSE LET'S FACE IT, WE ALL CONTRIBUTE TO POLLUTION SO WE ALL MUST WORK TOGETHER TO FIND A SOLUTION...

"I'LL LOOK FORWARD TO THAT DAY."

It's freezing cold.

(I could be at home...)

GREENPEACE CLIMATE CHANGE PROTEST.

A BP OIL RIG, STATIONED IN THE CROMARTY FIRTH.

DEPTHS

DEVELOPED WITH	WRITTEN BY	ART BY	COLORS BY	LETTERING BY
MEENA RAJPUT	COREY BROTHERSON	GERALDO BORGES	LEE LOUGHRIDGE	BERNARDO BRICE

This drilling rig ladder is about 30 meters tall.

Even at my current height, a fall into the water could badly injure me. That's if I don't hit anything on the way down.

(...in the warmth...)

I know I can do this. I've been at Greenpeace for over six years now. I'm trained for this.

(...cozy and watching Netflix.)

Why are you doing this, Meena?

I've been asked "Can't someone else do it?"

No. No matter the cold. No matter the difficulty. No.

Stop looking away--

--and start looking up.

Look at *everything* around us. Our society. Our environment. *Us.*

Change only starts and ends with us.

My family always says: "Bad things never happen when you try."

CLIMATE EMERGENCY

So I'm always going to keep trying.

On 14th June 2019, Meena and her Greenpeace UK co-protester Andrew climbed and chained themselves to the Transocean/BP oil rig, Paul B Loyd Junior. Between them and six others, they occupied the rig for a combined total of almost six days.

Their actions prevented the rig from leaving the North Sea to the Vorlich oil field, helping raise awareness of the injustices and dangers of fossil fuel drilling during a mounting climate emergency.

Meena continues to work at Greenpeace as an activist, while also focusing on establishing an anti-racist culture through action and her own children's books.

COMMUNITY AND CULTURE
BY MEENA RAJPUT

Think about it like this: Would governments and corporations still drag their heels with climate solutions if it were their richest citizens who were suffering the consequences of climate change? Hurricanes, droughts, flooding on a daily basis? NO, they wouldn't.

Yet hundreds of thousands of people of colour and Indigenous communities around the world are experiencing, death, displacement and suffering caused by environmental destruction and climate related disasters.

Despite knowing this, governments and corporations do very little to change their policies and business models - business models that directly cause climate change and are built on histories of human exploitation. They know it must stop, but they continue driven by greed, while silencing the solutions proposed by impacted communities. As well as causing social injustice, they have disrupted the climate and nature to the point of threatening humanity's existence.

We all have a choice. We can continue accepting the way things are or we fight for change.

Change will come if we all suppport and join communities fighting for a better world, if communities unite with one another, and if we promote a culture of justice and equality.

WHAT YOU CAN DO TO HELP:

1. Connect and act in solidarity with communities fighting for change.

2. Think of ways you can tackle systemic inequality and the climate crisis.

3. Take action together and influence leaders to drive change.

A CLIMATE OF HOPE

DEVELOPED WITH	ADAPTED BY	ART & COLORS BY	LETTERING BY
PROF. MICHAEL MANN	ROGER STERN	JOE ORSAK	JIM CAMPBELL

"IT IS ALL OF THE THINGS WE HAVE TALKED ABOUT--

"BEHAVIORAL CHANGE,

PUT CARBON TO GOOD USE
PLANT A TREE

"INCENTIVIZED BY APPROPRIATE GOVERNMENT POLICY,

"INTERGOVERNMENTAL AGREEMENTS,

"AND TECHNOLOGICAL INNOVATION--

"THAT WILL LEAD US FORWARD ON CLIMATE. IT IS NOT ANY ONE OF THESE THINGS, BUT ALL OF THEM WORKING TOGETHER, AT THIS UNIQUE MOMENT IN HISTORY, THAT PROVIDES TRUE REASON FOR HOPE.

"TO REPEAT ONE OF THE EPIGRAPHS THAT BEGAN THIS FINAL CHAPTER, 'HOPE IS A GOOD THING, MAYBE THE BEST OF THINGS.' ALONE IT WON'T SOLVE THIS PROBLEM. BUT DRAWING UPON IT, WE WILL."

Michael E. Mann

PROJECT MILESTONES

£1,000,000
Help fund our global oceans campaign for a year.

£500,000
Support world-class scientific research on wildlife ecosystems.

£100,000
Enable us to lobby decision-makers to agree to a Global Oceans Treaty.

£50,000
Provide resources to investigate destructive fishing practices.

GREENPEACE

THE MONEY WE RAISE IS HELPING:

SECURE GLOBAL OCEAN PROTECTION

The oceans are home to incredible wildlife, provide food for billions and help balance our climate; yet only a tiny fraction is protected. For decades humans have plundered and polluted this precious environment. We urgently need to establish a global network of ocean sanctuaries to help our oceans recover.

WHY IS THE PROJECT SO IMPORTANT?

Our fate is bound to the fate of our oceans. They do more than harbor incredible wildlife—they support all life on Earth. By producing half our oxygen and soaking up huge amounts of carbon dioxide, oceans are one of our best defenses against climate change. If they don't make it, we don't, either.

Protecting our oceans needs international cooperation. Greenpeace is campaigning around the world to persuade governments to agree to a strong Global Ocean Treaty at the United Nations. This is an historic opportunity to create ocean sanctuaries, areas safe from human exploitation, across at least 30% of our oceans by 2030.

Wherever a proper ocean sanctuary is created, the results are dramatic. Habitats recover. The fish come back. Life finds a way. A global network of sanctuaries is a brilliantly simple—and achievable—solution to some of the threats our oceans face.

SPECIES PROFILE

Every year thousands of turtles are caught in industrial fishing nets and their feeding grounds and breeding habits are threatened by climate change. Most species face extinction. Protected areas will give sea turtles and other marine life the chance they need to recover and thrive.

> " **We need to protect the ocean as if our lives depend on it, because they do.** "
>
> Dr. Sylvia A. Earle, marine biologist, explorer, and author

BURU SEA, INDONESIA
Handline fishing on Buru Island.

PROJECT IN ACTION

This project will inspire millions around the world to add their voices to the campaign, such as during this World Oceans Day Event in Mexico. It will support leading scientists to deliver new research, making the case for global oceans protection. And it will put pressure on decision-makers at the highest levels of government.

THE FUTURE

If we succeed, this global network of ocean sanctuaries will be one of the biggest conservation efforts in human history, creating millions of square kilometers of new protected areas. Ocean life would become healthier, more abundant, and better able to cope with big global threats like climate change and plastic pollution.

FIND OUT MORE
SIGN THE PETITION: HTTP://GREENPEACE.ORG.UK/PROTECT-THE-OCEANS
FIND OUT MORE: HTTPS://WWW.GREENPEACE.ORG.UK/CHALLENGES/OCEAN-SANCTUARIES/

CHAPTER TWO
PROTECT
THE WORLD

Currently, our most precious and biodiverse areas are under attack. From business exploitation to fishing waste, mining to illegal wildlife trade, the threats are numerous but the solution is simple...

Often this land is occupied by Indigenous communities who daily face the harsh realities of external commercial land-use change on the delicate ecosystems they have respected for generations. And when these incredible pockets of paradise are gone, we all suffer.

We are working with World Land Trust to buy some of the most important land on Earth, and gift it back to the indigenous communities who live there, safeguarding it for those who have proven time and time again to be the best stewards of it.

Sponsored project:

WORLD
LAND
TRUST

THE SHEPHERD & THE THUNDER

THERE IS A PROVISION IN THE UNITED NATIONS WORLD CHARTER FOR NATURE THAT CALLS ON NONGOVERNMENTAL GROUPS TO ASSIST IN SAFEGUARDING NATURE IN AREAS BEYOND NATIONAL JURISDICTION.

DEVELOPED WITH
PETER HAMMARSTEDT
WRITTEN BY
BRIAN AZZARELLO
ART & COLORS BY
DANIJEL ZEZELJ
LETTERING BY
BERNARDO BRICE

THE *THUNDER.*

GLOBALLY THE MOST NOTORIOUS PIRATE FISHING VESSEL, WAS SINKING OFF THE COAST OF NIGERIA.

MOST LIKELY SCUTTLED BY ITS OWN CREW.

IN THE PAST DECADE, THE THUNDER HAD COLLECTED OVER **$76 MILLION** FROM ILLICIT SALES OF TOOTHFISH-- AKA CHILEAN SEA BASS.

THE THUNDER HAD BEEN BANNED FROM FISHING SINCE 2006.

FOR SEA SHEPHERD CAPTAIN **PETER HAMMARSTEDT,** A MAN WHO'D DOGGEDLY CHASED THE THUNDER FOR ONE HUNDRED AND TEN DAYS THROUGH TWO SEAS AND THREE OCEANS, THE ENDING WAS BITTERSWEET.

PETER IS A MEMBER OF **SEA SHEPHERD,** A MARINE CONSERVATION ORGANIZATION THAT ENGAGES IN DIRECT ACTIONS TO DEFEND WILDLIFE AND PROTECT THE OCEANS FROM ILLEGAL EXPLOITATION.

SEA SHEPHERD DESCRIBES ITSELF AS AN **ECO-VIGILANTE** GROUP.

HE'D IMAGINED IT DIFFERENTLY. BRINGING THE THUNDER TO PORT, TO STAND TRIAL FOR CRIMES, AND A BLATANT DISREGARD FOR THE WORLD'S BIODIVERSITY.

ILLEGAL FISHING GENERATES $100 BILLION ANNUALLY.

BUT THE ACTUAL COSTS TO LIFE IS MUCH HIGHER.

IN THEIR GREEDY PURSUITS, ILLEGAL NETS WERE USED-- NETS THAT DIDN'T JUST HAUL IN "TODAY'S CATCH", BUT *BYCATCH* AS WELL.

"BYCATCH" BEING A BLOODLESS TERM FOR A FISH OR OTHER MARINE SPECIES THAT IS CAUGHT UNINTENTIONALLY WHILE CATCHING CERTAIN TARGET SPECIES.

IT WASN'T JUST SEA-LIFE THAT WAS IMPACTED, EITHER. LOCAL FISHERMEN WERE BEING FORCED FURTHER FROM SHORE BY ILLEGAL OVERFISHING. THE WATERS WERE *DANGEROUS*...

AND SOMETIMES *WORSE*.

BUT IN THE GABONESE PORT, CAPTAIN HAMMARSTEDT MET LIKE-MINDED INDIVIDUALS. A GOVERNMENT THAT HAD THE WAYS, BUT NOT THE MEANS, TO COMBAT MARINE POACHING.

ALL THEY NEEDED WAS A *BOAT*.

SEA SHEPHERD PROVIDES THE SHIPS, THE CREW, AND THE FUEL.

GOVERNMENT PARTNERS PROVIDE THE LAW ENFORCEMENT TO BOARD, INSPECT, AND ARREST ANY VIOLATORS OF THE LAW.

SO, ONE ENDING LEADS TO A BEGINNING. BUT THAT'S WHAT **PASSION** IS, ISN'T IT?

THE THUNDER MAY HAVE **SUNK**, BUT THE BOB BARKER* IS STILL ON **PATROL**.

BECAUSE DEEP SEA SHARK POPULATIONS HAVE BEEN DECIMATED BY 80%.

BECAUSE THE DEATHS OF 300,000 WHALES AND DOLPHINS PER YEAR IS DUE TO BYCATCH.

BECAUSE OVER 50% OF THE WORLD'S MAJOR FISHING GROUNDS HAVE BEEN DEPLETED.

SEA SHEPHERD HAS ASSISTED IN ARRESTING 65 ILLEGAL POACHING VESSELS OFF THE COAST OF AFRICA.

BOB BARKER

* The Bob Barker is named after the former host of *The Price Is Right*, who generously supported their cause.

To learn what you can do to help, or discover more about the Sea Shepherd's mission, visit www.seashepherd.org

SAIKOU'S NIGHTMARE AND A DREAM

KARTONG, GAMBIA.

AFTER A WHOLE DAY FISHING, IT'S ALWAYS GOOD TO BE HOME.

DEVELOPED WITH
MUSTAPHA MANNEH & SAINEY GIBBA
WRITTEN AND PENCILLED BY
ABDULKAREEM BABA AMINU
INKS AND COLORS BY | LETTERING BY
RYAN CODY | **BERNARDO BRICE**

REST, DINNER, AND AISHA: HOME IS WHERE EVERYTHING IS. WELL, ALMOST EVERYTHING.

WELCOME HOME, SAIKOU. LET ME TAKE YOUR BAG.

THANK YOU, DEAR WIFE. YOU'RE FAR TOO KIND.

I'M AFRAID THERE'S NO FISH TODAY EITHER, MY DEAR...

DON'T BE SILLY. I JUST WANT TO AIR OUT YOUR WORK CLOTHES.

GOOD NIGHT.

SLEEP WELL.

I SLEEP...

...AND IT'S THE SAME NIGHTMARE AS THE NIGHT BEFORE.

Gambia has three fishmeal factories operating on the coastline communities. All three are Chinese owned, and their practices have destroyed local fishing trade and resulted in the pollution of our local waters and fish.

They process massive amounts of raw fish into fishmeal and oil, the scale of which is causing a national disaster for the people of Gambia.

ANOTHER NIGHTMARE?

YES.

SADLY, MY NIGHTMARE IS ALSO OUR REALITY.

BUT LIKE EVERY OTHER DAY OR NIGHT, I HAVE HOPE THAT THINGS WILL GET BETTER TODAY.

SAIKOU'S NIGHTMARE — AND HIS DREAM — AREN'T HIS ALONE.

THEY'RE OURS.

WHAT DID YOU WISH FOR?

HETTIE HAD JUST TURNED THIRTEEN WHEN HER PARENTS SENT HER OFF TO SAILING CAMP.

IN 1991, MOUNT PINATUBO ERUPTED, MAKING MIGRANTS OF MANY IN THE PHILIPPINES.

AT FIRST, THE LOGIC OF SAILING ELUDED HER.

WHAT HAPPENS WHEN THE WIND IS NOT BLOWING WHERE YOU WANT TO GO?

THE WIND IS INVISIBLE, BUT HER EFFECTS ARE NOT.

IF YOU UNDERSTAND HER STRENGTH AND HER DIRECTION, SHE CAN TAKE YOU ANYWHERE...

THE U.S. MILITARY ABANDONED THEIR MILITARY BASES, LEAVING BEHIND A SHELTER AND A TOXIC LEGACY.

BUT LIFE BROKE THROUGH IN THAT SPACE...

...A SAILOR WAS BORN.

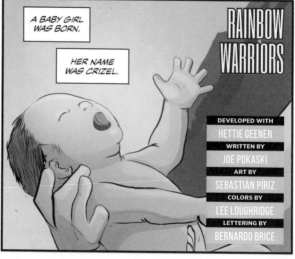

A BABY GIRL WAS BORN.

HER NAME WAS CRIZEL.

RAINBOW WARRIORS

DEVELOPED WITH
HETTIE GEENEN
WRITTEN BY
JOE POKASKI
ART BY
SEBASTIÁN PÍRIZ
COLORS BY
LEE LOUGHRIDGE
LETTERING BY
BERNARDO BRICE

IF YOU LOOK TO THE LEFT, YOU CAN SEE THE ORIGINAL PORT, WHICH BACK IN THE DAY...

HETTIE STUCK WITH SAILING, WORKING ON A CHARTER CIRCUIT FOR TOURISTS.

THE POISONS OF THE PAST SEEPED INTO THE LIVES OF EVERYONE WHO LIVED THERE.

CRIZEL WAS NO EXCEPTION.

BY THE TIME HER 30TH BIRTHDAY ROLLED AROUND, HETTIE WAS HOPING TO FIND MORE DIRECTION IN HER OWN SAILS.

WHAT DID YOU WISH FOR?

I'M TOLD THERE IS A DRAWING CONTEST COMING UP. WOULD YOU BE INTERESTED?

YOU KNOW HOW MUCH I LOVE TO DRAW, MAMA.

HETTIE FOUND IT-- WHEN HER FRIEND TOLD HER ABOUT GREENPEACE, AND A SHIP.

IT WAS LIKE SOMETHING FROM A DREAM.

RAINBOW WARRIOR

IT'S BEAUTIFUL... DOES IT HAVE A NAME?

"THE RAINBOW WARRIOR."

IT WAS CRIZEL'S DREAM, TO SEE THE BOAT, TO UNDERSTAND WHAT HOPE LOOKED LIKE. TO HOPE IT COULD SAVE THE WORLD.

AND IT WAS SEEING THIS SHIP THROUGH THIS YOUNG GIRL'S EYES THAT HELPED HETTIE SEE HER LIFE MORE CLEARLY.

ARE YOU GOING TO MAKE A WISH?

"THE WIND IS INVISIBLE, BUT HER EFFECTS ARE NOT.

"IF YOU UNDERSTAND HER STRENGTH AND HER DIRECTION, SHE CAN TAKE YOU ANYWHERE..."

THE END

WRITTEN AND DRAWN BY
VICTOR SOLÍS

THE SELFLESS GIANT

DEVELOPED WITH **ANDY SERKIS** | WRITTEN BY **PAUL GOODENOUGH** | ART & COLORS BY **DANIJEL ZEZELJ** | LETTERING BY **BERNARDO BRICE**

WE ARE LOSING ARTIC ICE AT THE RATE OF 13% PER DECADE.
IF WE CONTINUE AT THIS RATE, EARTH COULD BE ICE FREE BY 2040.

THIS STORY IS DEDICATED TO THE SELFLESS GIANT GLACIERS THAT KEPT US SAFE FOR SO LONG.
WE ARE SORRY. WE WILL DO BETTER. WE HAVE TO.

School's Out

WRITTEN AND DRAWN BY
WAR AND PEAS

War and Peas

WRITTEN BY	ART BY
TAIKA WAITITI, PAUL GOODENOUGH AND SAFELY ENDANGERED	SAFELY ENDANGERED

OHNO

© 2021 AZZ + CHIANG (AFTER KELLY)

WRITTEN BY **BRIAN AZZARELLO**   ART & LETTERING BY **CLIFF CHIANG**

SHO' IS *LONELY* BEIN' ALL BY MY *LONESOME.*

U.S.S. TP MINE

I BEEN *THINKIN'*--

I *THOUGHT* I SMELLED SOMETHIN' *BURNIN'.*

THAT MUST BE THE *WILDFIRES.*

THEM AGIN? ALL *I'M* SMELLIN' IS A *SEA LEVEL* ROSE.

WELP, PASSED ALL THEM *EEKOLOGY* LAWS, BUT WAS THE *FILLIN' STATIONS* THEY *DIN'* PASS DONE US IN.

FOSSIL FUEL, REPORTIN' FER DUTY, SIR.

GOOD TO HAVE YOU, MY PRIVATES, FOR THE *WAR* IS *LOST.*

WHAT'S EATIN' YA, OHNO?

AIN' YOU, GATOR.

WELL, NO, I LOST ME MY APPLETIGHT, ONCE I CAUGHT ME THE STINKSHUN.

YOU CAUGHT THE STINKSHUN? HOW LONG WAS YOU DOWN WITH IT?

FER THE COUNT, FRIEN'. DOWN FER THE COUNT.

TWIXT THE OCEANS AN' INFERNOS, OKEFENOKEE HURLED 'TWEEN THE WAVES.

AW, YOU MAKE IT SOUN' SO NICE.

SO SAD! DEM SCIENCES YOU SPOUTIN' JUS' FAKE NEWS! THIS HERE IS JUS' MOTHER NATURE, NOT A LACK OF HUMAN NURTURE!

TWEET TWEET TWEET

WHAT?!?

YES...

WE HAVE MET THE ENEMY, AND THEY IS YOU.

Important Takeaway

WRITTEN BY **STEVE BACKSHALL** | ART & LETTERING BY **HARRY VENNING**

BY PETER HAMMARSTEDT

Sea Shepherd Captain of the *Bob Barker*. Illustration by Steve White

Over fifty years ago, the French ocean explorer Jacques Cousteau said that:

"

THE OCEANS ARE IN DANGER OF DYING

Since then, the number of fish in the world's oceans has been halved; shark and ray populations have fallen by **70%** since 1970.

Considering that illegal, unreported and unregulated (IUU) fishing is responsible for **20%** of the global fishing catch, shutting down illegal fishing operations is critical to turning the tide of destruction facing the oceans.

HOW CAN YOU HELP?

- Consider switching to a plant-based diet.

- Lobby government to end fishing subsidies that currently amount to over **$35 billion** per year.

- Push for the creation of no-catch marine protected areas with the goal of conserving **30%** of the oceans by 2030.

- Support Sea Shepherd's efforts to conduct joint at-sea patrol with island and coastal States around the African continent, partnerships that have led to the arrest of **68** vessels for illegal fishing and other fisheries crime.

WRITTEN BY
DAVID SCHNEIDER, AMBER WEEDON AND SAFELY ENDANGERED

ART BY
SAFELY ENDANGERED

UNITED, OF ONE MIND AND PURPOSE...

... WE LOCATE THE SOURCE OF THE DANGER.

THE RED X SPELLS DEATH.

THE JENGI EXPLAINS IN THE DREAM-TONGUE...

SEE – THE TRAIL OF DEVASTATION WROUGHT BY THE INVADERS.

SEE – THE CALAMITOUS FOOTPRINT OF OUR ENEMY.

SEE – A WORLD PUSHED TO THE BRINK.

BUT IN UNITY THERE IS DEFIANCE.

TROPICAL FORESTS CONTAIN AT LEAST TWO-THIRDS OF EARTH'S BIODIVERSITY IN LESS THAN 10% OF ITS SURFACE AREA.

BY WORLD LAND TRUST AND RESERVA: THE YOUTH LAND TRUST
ILLUSTRATION BY NEIL BLACKBIRD SIMS

Home to hundreds of thousands of known species and millions more yet to be discovered or described by scientists, each patch of forest is as unique as the human fingerprint; once an area is lost, it can never be truly recovered. 28,400 acres, or 45 square miles, are lost every day.

In place of these botanical marvels, we install industrial-scale plantations of soy and palm oil, pastures for cattle, and mining operations of metals, oil, gas and timber.

But it's not too late.

The best tool to fight the combined threats of climate change and biodiversity loss is the conservation of tropical forests. As world leaders work on global goals to conserve 30% of the planet by 2030, what you do makes a difference.

1. REDUCE DEFORESTATION THROUGH EVERYDAY CHOICES

Eat locally sourced food, shop antiques before ordering new furniture, eat a plant-rich diet, divest from gold and oil, and get in the habit of asking the question, "Where did this come from?"

2. RESTORE LOCAL FORESTS

You may not live in the Amazon Rainforest, but your local ecosystem is almost certainly in need of help.
Volunteer with a local conservancy to plant native trees and remove invasive species.

3. PROTECT WHAT REMAINS

Organize fundraisers to protect habitat through organizations like the ones highlighted here. Whether you're an artist, a teacher, or you know some good jokes, you have skills that can be converted into acres of protected forest through creative fundraising.

TOGETHER WE CAN ENSURE THE WORLD'S TROPICAL PRIMARY FORESTS CONTINUE TO STAND TALL.
SAVE LAND. SAVE SPECIES. SAVE FORESTS

There's Blood On Your Hands

CHOCÓ RAINFOREST,
ECUADOR.

FRAGILE

WITH BIODIVERSIFICATION AND RESTORATION EFFORTS GAINING MORE
PUBLIC ATTENTION, THE CHOCÓ NEEDS HELP NOW MORE THAN EVER. THIS
ONCE-BOUNTIFUL RAINFOREST IS DOWN TO JUST 2% OF ITS FORMER
COVERAGE, WITH SEVERE WATER CONTAMINATION LEVELS ON THE RISE.
YOUR PURCHASE OF THIS BOOK WILL DIRECTLY BENEFIT RESERVA'S
CONSERVATION EFFORTS.

FIN

Barb and Rudy

WRITTEN AND DRAWN BY
THE PERRY BIBLE FELLOWSHIP

LOSS OF OUR LAND

WRITTEN AND DRAWN BY | **CONSULTING EXPERT**
ARIELA KRISTANTINA | BRADLEY HILLER

"THE FATE OF INDONESIA'S FORESTS AND PEATLANDS COULD MAKE OR BREAK THE WORLD'S GOAL TO LIMIT GLOBAL WARMING..."

— SIR NICHOLAS STERN.

WE LOST OUR SOURCES OF WATER...

OUR FOOD PERISHED.

PEOPLE ARE MAKING MONEY OFF OF OUR FOREST.

THE WORLD PROFITS. HUMANS PROFIT. BUT WE DON'T. WE LOSE. WE JUST... DIE.

THE UNITED NATIONS IDENTIFIES TROPICAL PEATLANDS ACROSS SOUTHEAST ASIA, AFRICA, THE CARIBBEAN, AND SOUTH AND CENTRAL AMERICA. THESE ECOSYSTEMS PROVIDE IMPORTANT CARBON SEQUESTRATION AND WATER REGULATION SERVICES, AS WELL AS SUPPORTING LOCAL LIVELIHOODS AND RICH BIODIVERSITY.

HOWEVER, TROPICAL PEATLANDS ARE INCREASINGLY VULNERABLE TO HUMAN- AND CLIMATE-INDUCED THREATS, INCLUDING DEFORESTATION, DRAINAGE, AND FIRE. GIVEN THAT MANY OF US GLOBALLY CONSUME PRODUCTS WHICH — DIRECTLY OR INDIRECTLY PLACE PRESSURES ON THESE SYSTEMS — FOR EXAMPLE, HALF OF PACKAGED PRODUCTS IN SUPERMARKETS TODAY CAN CONTAIN PALM OIL — WE HAVE A SHARED RESPONSIBILITY FOR THEIR SUSTAINABLE MANAGEMENT.

WHEN THESE FORESTS AND PEATLANDS ARE GONE, THE REST OF THE ECOSYSTEM WILL SOON FOLLOW. US INCLUDED.

FOREST HERO

INSPIRED BY
PAULO ADARIO
WRITTEN BY
DESIREE ALVARADO
ART BY
DAVID BAILLIE

MAY THE BEST ENDANGERED SPECIES WIN!

DEVELOPED WITH
CALLIE BROADDUS

WRITTEN BY
TYLER JENNES

ART AND LETTERING BY
SHEILA PUTRI

@SHEILASPLAYGROUND

GRANDMA'S AMAZING ADVENTURES

DEVELOPED WITH **MALAIKA VAZ** | WRITTEN BY **PAUL GOODENOUGH** | ART & LETTERING BY **MOMO & POPO**

JUST SHOOT US

WRITTEN BY
PAUL GOODENOUGH

ART & LETTERING BY
KEN CATALINO

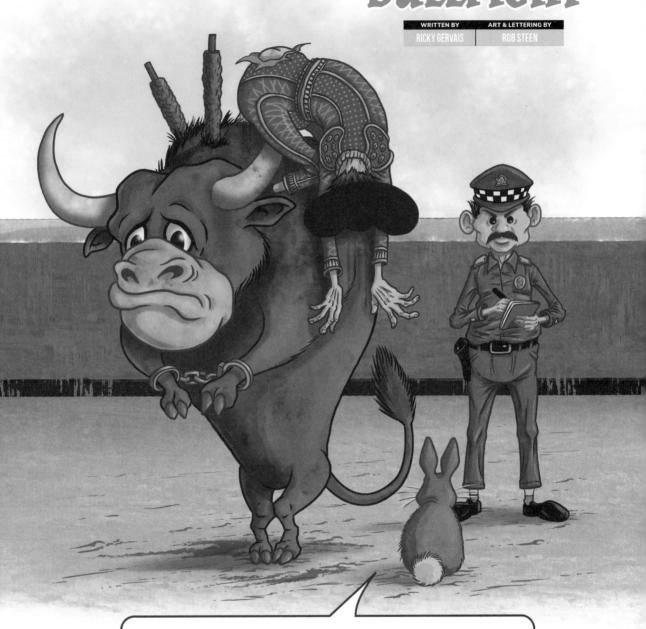

There's No One Like Me

WRITTEN AND DRAWN BY
SAD ANIMAL FACTS

sad animal facts

Woah! But does it hurt?

...

Hey, you know what?

If they move me again, or if ever you can't feel me near you...

♪ ...When you're here ♫
I'm not scared...

Mama Bear

DEVELOPED WITH	WRITTEN BY	ART & LETTERING BY
WORLD ANIMAL PROTECTION	JENNY JINYA & PAUL GOODENOUGH	JENNY JINYA

Thousands of bears are suffering in the bear bile industry. Forced to endure a lifetime in captivity, they are exploited for their bile — an ingredient used in some traditional medicines that is painfully extracted from the bears' gallbladder.

World Animal Protection is working to end bear bile farming. Together with other NGOs, local partners, and governments, they aim to change consumer behaviour, improve legislation and law enforcement, promote better welfare for captive bears, and strive to ensure no new bears enter the industry.

For more information visit:

www.worldanimalprotection.org.uk

EARTH DAY

WRITTEN AND DRAWN BY
DAMI LEE

WAAA-

#bestlife #livingthedream #goals #monkey
75 likes 54 shares

oh my gawd!!! ♥♥♥♥♥♥♥
2 mins Reply

soooo cuuuute!!! ♥♥♥♥♥♥♥
2 mins Reply

I WANT ONE!!! ♥♥♥♥♥♥♥
2 mins Reply

How beautiful! ♥♥♥♥♥♥@♥♥
2 mins Reply

Where did you get it??????? ♥♥♥
2 mins Reply

Liberia Chimpanzee Rescue & Protection is the first and **only** chimpanzee sanctuary and conservation center in Liberia.

Here they rescue and provide lifetime care to chimpanzees who are victims of the illegal bushmeat and pet trades.

And this is Ellie now, and this is her story of finding sanctuary.

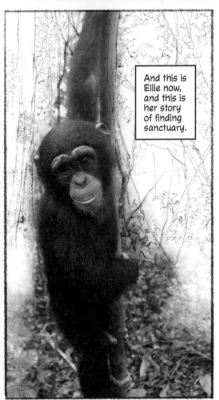

Wise Tree

WRITTEN AND DRAWN BY
WAR AND PEAS

War and Peas

WRITTEN AND DRAWN BY
DINOS AND COMICS

dinos and comics

His name is **P-22**. He rules the Hollywood Hills. And he's the most famous mountain lion in the world.

BRIDGE TO THE FUTURE

WRITTEN BY
RUTH FLETCHER GAGE & CHRISTOS GAGE

ART BY
MIKE PERKINS

LETTERING BY
BERNARDO BRICE

HOLLYWOOD

He has his own social media accounts, merchandise, even plush toys.

But like too many true Hollywood stories, there's a tragedy underneath the glitz and glamour.

P-22 is alone.

Griffith Park, where P-22 lives, is surrounded by freeways. It has no native population of mountain lions.

Surrounding mountain ranges do. And when cougar cubs grow up, their instinct is to find their own territory. But when they try to cross a freeway...

...it doesn't end well.

P-22 crossed **two** freeways. He's famous because he survived-- something no other big cat had. He's got prey, territory, and fame.

But he has no one to share it with.

But there's a way to **change** that. They're called **Wildlife Corridors**.

Bridges or tunnels designed for animals to get past freeways without risking being hit by cars.

They've already succeeded in other parts of the country and the world.

A bridge in Utah went viral thanks to a YouTube video of all the animals using it.

India and Africa have built massive elephant corridors.

The short-term benefit is the safety of both animals and humans. The long-term benefit...

...is love.

And genetic diversity. When a small population of animals--like the cougars in the Santa Monica Mountains--is confined to one place, inbreeding occurs.

The lack of mates causes birth defects, like crooked tails...and eventually more serious problems that could lead to extinction.

A wildlife corridor would also allow a wider range of animals, like P-22 and the Santa Monica lions, to mingle, promoting genetic diversity and strong offspring. (Adorable, too.)

Of course, these cost money. The Liberty Canyon Wildlife Crossing would span L.A.'s 101 Freeway. They hope to break ground soon, with a 2023 completion date.

You can help, by donating at SaveLACougars.org. Or find a wildlife corridor project near you that could use a hand.

If enough of us chip in, we can give P-22 the Hollywood ending he deserves.

BORN FREE FOREVER

DEVELOPED WITH	WRITTEN BY	ART & COLORS BY	LETTERING BY
VIRGINIA MCKENNA OBE	TAB MURPHY	MWELWA TAX	JIM CAMPBELL

FATHER? IS EVERYTHING OKAY?

I WAS JUST THINKING ABOUT YOUR GREAT-GREAT-GREAT-GRANDMOTHER.

"WE'VE BEEN PERSECUTED AND HUNTED...

"OUR HABITAT LOST...

"OUR NATURAL PREY DEPLETED...

Dedicated to Elsa the Lioness.

'Who will care for the animals for they cannot look after themselves? Are there young men and women willing to take on this charge? Who will raise their voices to plead their case when mine is carried away on the wind?'

George Adamson 1906 - 1989

DR. CAROLINE NG'WENO

VIRGINIA McKENNA

DAVID MANOA

RAABIA HAWA

BELLA LACK

'BORN FREE FOREVER'

Hedgehog Heroes!

INSPIRED BY
MICHAEL ROSEN

WRITTEN BY
HUGH WARWICK

ART & LETTERING BY
STIG

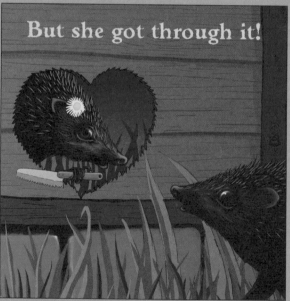

Help hedgehogs find love - Make holes in your fences!
Create a Hedgehog Street

What if God was one of us...

INSPIRED AND LYRICS BY	WRITTEN AND DRAWN BY
ERIC BAZILIAN	ALICIA SOUZA

SHARED EXPERIENCES

STORY INSPIRED BY	WRITTEN AND DRAWN BY
PAUL, MARY, AND STELLA MCCARTNEY AND MEAT FREE MONDAY	JUST COMICS

Never Forget

DEVELOPED WITH	WRITTEN BY	ART & LETTERING BY
BROOKLYN BECKHAM AND WORLD ANIMAL PROTECTION	PAUL GOODENOUGH	BUDDY GATOR

END WILDLIFE CRIME

BY JOHN SCANLON. ILLUSTRATION BY MISTER HOPE.

Hundreds of thousands of wild animals and plants are trafficked every year, from pangolins to elephants, orchids to rosewood, eels to sharks.

During the last decade, more than **a million pangolins** were trafficked, with more than **128 tons** of their scales and meat seized by the authorities in just one year.

An astonishing **1.7 million** undiscovered viruses are thought to exist in animals living in the wild, half of which could spill over to people, and this could be devastating for our health—yet, the numbers of trafficked wild animals keep rising at alarming levels.

Wildlife trafficking drives species toward extinction, decimates ecosystems and their ability to sequester carbon, results in governments being deprived of revenue, and leads to more corruption, insecurity and poverty.

The impact of these crimes on ecosystems adds up to a gargantuan **$1–2 trillion** a year in value.

HELP KEEP WILDLIFE IN THE WILD!

1. Be careful what you buy, and never buy animals as pets that have been taken from the wild. Let wildlife remain in its natural habitat.

2. Share this message—tell your friends and family about the devastating destruction that wildlife trafficking is causing.

3. Voice the importance of scaling up wildlife law enforcement to politicians and the world so we can end wildlife crime.

£250,000
Tackle pangolin
trafficking in
Eastern India,
and fight the loss
of biodiversity
caused by the
international
wildlife trade.

£50,000
African Lions:
Protect community
livestock and
prevent predator
revenge attacks in
Southern Kenya.

£25,000
Eastern Lowland
Gorilla: Collaborate
with the Pole Pole
Foundation in DRC,
and protect
elephants and
giraffes in Northern
Kenya.

£10,000
Raise the Red Flag:
Expose the
negative human
exploitation of all
wild animals
globally.

THE MONEY WE RAISE IS HELPING:

KEEP WILDLIFE IN THE WILD

With nearly four decades of experience, Born Free cares for and conserves some of the world's most iconic, yet persecuted, wild animal species, safeguards habitats, empowers local communities, and inspires current and future generations to look after all life on Earth and keep wildlife in the wild.

WHY IS THE PROJECT SO IMPORTANT?

Every project Born Free undertakes is vitally important. Exposing the brutal impact of the international wildlife trade on endangered species; protecting Eastern lowland gorillas and their habitat; helping communities safeguard their livestock and, thereby, preventing the killing of threatened lions; working with communities to conserve wild tigers; spearheading landscape-level efforts to protect ecosystems, such as the Dja Biosphere Reserve in Cameroon and the iconic species that live there. Our unique approach, which we call compassionate conservation, places the welfare of individual wild animals at the heart of our strategies and actions. Our milestones are ambitious, practical, and transformative.

Each milestone we reach, each successfully funded project, will enable Born Free to increase our support for key wildlife species; enhance our engagement with local communities; apply effective, innovative solutions; and tackle the many pressures facing wildlife and our natural world.

SPECIES PROFILES

Wild orangutans are threatened by habitat loss, illegal hunting, and trade in infants as "pets." Just 20,000 African lions remain in the wild today, down 80% in fifty years. In the last decade, more than one million wild pangolins have been poached for meat and scales.

> " The natural world is vulnerable, as never before. It's time for compassionate, caring individuals to come together and protect all that we hold dear. "
>
> Virginia McKenna, OBE co-founder. The Born Free Foundation

AMBOSELI, KENYA 📍
One elephant is killed for its tusks every twenty minutes.

THE FUTURE

Every project we undertake helps Born Free secure a better future for iconic species—lions, tigers, elephant, rhino, gorillas, chimpanzees, orangutans, pangolins, giraffes, and more. We always treat individual wild animals with respect and compassion, as part of functional, viable ecosystems.

FIND OUT MORE

> SIGN UP AT WWW.BORNFREE.ORG.UK TO GET THE LATEST NEWS ABOUT OUR WORK AND HOW YOU CAN HELP DELIVERED STRAIGHT TO YOUR INBOX.
> FOLLOW BORN FREE FOUNDATION ON SOCIAL MEDIA FOR CONTINUOUS UPDATES ON OUR AWARD-WINNING CONSERVATION WORK.

PROJECT IN ACTION

Born Free has built more than 330 "predator-proof bomas" that protect the livestock of pastoral communities at night. If their cattle, sheep, and goats are safe, local people tolerate lions and other predators. So far we have helped more than 6,000 people, 80,000 head of livestock—and the wild predators of southern Kenya.

Plastic trash is found in 90 percent of seabirds, revealed in a new study*.

"Plastic found inside birds includes bags, bottle caps, synthetic fibers from clothing, and tiny rice-sized bits that have been broken down by the sun and waves. The study found a 67 percent decline in seabird populations between 1950 and 2010. Albatross are more prone to eating plastic because they fish by skimming their beaks across the top of the water, and inadvertently take in plastics floating on the surface."

Sources:

https://www.nationalgeographic.com/news/2015/09/15092-plastic-seabirds-albatross-australia/

*https://www.pnas.org/content/early/2015/08/27/1502108112

Little Mo

WRITTEN AND DRAWN BY
JENNY JINYA

WRITTEN AND DRAWN BY
BUDDY GATOR

TORN

DEVELOPED WITH **KIDS AGAINST PLASTIC** ART AND WRITTEN BY **AMY MEEK**

IT STARTED WITH A PICTURE.

IT SHOOK ME TO MY CORE.

THE MASSIVE WASTE MANAGEMENT PROBLEM IN MY HOME, INDIA.

I HAD TO TAKE THE PROBLEM ON. AT THE *SOURCE*.

THE POWER OF YOUTH

DEVELOPED WITH
ADITYA MUKARJI
WRITTEN BY
ALEX SEGURA
ART & COLORS BY
GEORGE KAMBADAIS
LETTERING BY
JIM CAMPBELL

I WAS A CHILD, THOUGH. WHAT CAN A CHILD REALLY DO?

A LOT, I LEARNED.

THEN I MOVED INTO RAISING PUBLIC AWARENESS. I HELPED OTHERS LEARN WHAT THEY COULD DO.

WHAT, SO NO STRAWS?

JUST GIVE IT A TRY. *TRUST* ME.

THE YOUTH ARE INTEGRAL. THEY HAVE MORE EMOTION.

THEY DELIVER THE MESSAGE WITH *PASSION* AND *HONESTY.*

WHY EVEN GIVE OUT STRAWS? IT'S HURTING OUR PLANET.

I'M JUST TRYING TO DO MY--

LET ME TALK TO THE BOSS, OKAY? THIS IS IMPORTANT.

AND ADULTS *LISTEN.*

REFUSE IF YOU CANNOT REUSE. LEAVE THE WORLD A LITTLE BETTER THAN YOU FOUND IT.

NEVER BE AFRAID TO CHALLENGE THE STATUS QUO.

ALWAYS AIM HIGHER THAN YOUR TARGET.

million

Around the planet, children have been responsible for removing more than 30 million pieces of plastic from the environment.

#savetheplanet

£1,000,000
Would allow FUNDAECO to purchase and protect 1,788 acres (723.5 hectares) of the Laguna Grande Reserve. The protected area will provide habitat for the jaguar.

£100,000
Purchase and protect 178 acres (72 hectares) of the Laguna Grande Reserve. The protected area will provide habitat for the Baird's tapir.

£50,000
Purchase and protect 89 acres (36 hectares) of the Laguna Grande Reserve. The protected area will provide habitat for the Yucatan black howler monkey.

£10,000
Purchase and protect 17 acres (6.8 hectares) of the Laguna Grande Reserve. The protected area will provide habitat for the margay.

WORLD
LAND
TRUST

THE MONEY WE RAISE IS HELPING:

GUATEMALA'S LAGUNA GRANDE RESERVE

Acting as a natural water filter, flood barrier, and carbon sink, mangroves play a crucial role in ecosystems the world over. In Caribbean Guatemala, the 316,000-acre Laguna Grande project does all this and more, tackling the climate and biodiversity crises while providing sustainable livelihoods for local Indigenous communities.

WHY IS THE PROJECT SO IMPORTANT?

Landscapes like Laguna Grande bring benefits to conservation, communities, and climate, but without the proper protection these vital services could be lost forever. Supporters of Laguna Grande can help to preserve this vast and vitally important habitat, preventing the draining and deforestation that comes with unchecked development.

This is an ecosystem that captures and stores huge amounts of carbon, helping us win the fight against climate change. It also harbors iconic species like the jaguar, Baird's tapir, and West Indian manatee, and defends one of the world's most climate-vulnerable nations from natural disasters. Meanwhile, project partner FUNDAECO work tirelessly to support sustainable livelihoods and provide health services to communities.

This project will support the expansion of the Laguna Grande Reserve, protecting an additional 3,294 acres (1,333 hectares) of forest. Threatened by timber extraction, the forest is part of the Mesoamerican Biological Corridor, home to more than 350 bird species.

SPECIES PROFILE

Maintaining connectivity between habitats is critical for far-ranging predators like the jaguar, and this is exactly what purchasing land in Laguna Grande will achieve. Bringing more land under protection will allow rangers to expand their patrols, keeping the Americas' iconic big cat safe from poachers.

> **"** *The money that is given to the World Land Trust, in my estimation, has more effect on the wild world than almost anything I can think of.* **"**
>
> Sir David Attenborough, World Land Trust patron

LAGUNA GRANDE, GUATEMALA 📍

A mosaic of lagoons, mangroves, reefs, and tropical forests, Laguna Grande is a prime example of a thriving wetland ecosystem.

PROJECT IN ACTION

Project funds are utilized on the ground by FUNDAECO, a conservation organization that has worked in the area for more than twenty years. The management of Laguna Grande is conducted in partnership with local Indigenous association Amantes de la Tierra.

THE FUTURE

By protecting much-needed habitat for threatened species and providing a natural solution to the climate crisis, the success of Laguna Grande will help change the world for the better. With benefits shared between people and wildlife, the project can also offer a blueprint for future conservation initiatives in Guatemala and beyond.

FIND OUT MORE
> VISIT: WWW.WORLDLANDTRUST.ORG/WHAT-WE-DO/CARBON-BALANCED
> VISIT: WWW.WORLDLANDTRUST.ORG/APPEALS/ACTION-FUND

CHAPTER THREE
RESTORE
THE DAMAGE

We're working with five charities to undertake specific, targeted projects across the globe to undo some of the catastrophic damage done to the planet.

From rewilding, to species reintroduction and restoration, our project will put species back into recovery, enabling them to look after themselves, forever.

Sponsored projects:

EXPLORING MY OPTIONS

DEVELOPED WITH
KARRUECHE TRAN AND RE:WILD

WRITTEN AND DRAWN BY
ZACH STAFFORD

Rewild
the Galapagos

In the Galapagos Islands, people are intertwined with the wildlife and natural world surrounding them. Finches will land on your hand, while iguanas scurry past your feet, but not everything is perfect in paradise.

Local communities have seen animals they cherish disappear before their eyes, and more are teetering on the brink of extinction. Luckily, there is still time to reverse course.

We can and will rewild the Galapagos. It has become my life's mission to restore islands and reintroduce native animals, working alongside local communities to create ecosystems where people and wildlife thrive together.

The more people who know and support us, the more species we can save from extinction.

With love and hope. Paula A. Castaño

Art by Ian Stopforth   re:wild   ISLAND CONSERVATION
Preventing Extinctions

£250,000
Will pay for a predator-free sanctuary for Tasmanian devils and other native wildlife of East Australia to restore the ecological functioning of native forest ecosystems.

£100,000
Will pay for the build of a first-of-its-kind conservation breeding center for unique and threatened species of the Annamite Mountains.

£50,000
Feed and care for twenty Tasmanian devils for an entire year in a conservation breeding program to bring the Tasmanian devils back to mainland Australia.

£10,000
Supports a community member to remove snares from Pu Mat National Park in Vietnam for three years.

THE MONEY WE RAISE IS HELPING:

REWILD OUR WORLD!

The most effective solution to the triple threat of climate chaos, mass extinction, and emerging diseases is to protect and restore Earth's most irreplaceable places for biodiversity. We don't need to reinvent the planet, we just need to rewild it!

WHY IS THE PROJECT SO IMPORTANT?

This project will recover and restore critical wild areas, with a focus on two unique ecosystems critical to our global biodiversity.

In the forests of East Australia, damaged ecosystems have been ravaged by fires. We are embarking on a plan to restore lost ecosystems one species at a time. Starting with the Tasmanian devil, which we are working with our partners to bring to mainland Australia after a three-thousand-year absence. Devils allow native small mammals to recover by keeping invasive cats and foxes in check. By burying leaf litter as they forage, these small mammals help sustain cooler and less damaging fires.

In the rugged Annamite Mountains of Vietnam and Laos roams an animal that no living scientist has spotted in the wild. We are working to bring the saola back from the brink to resume its place among a wondrous assemblage of unique species through an innovative conservation breeding program to rewild one of the most biodiverse corners of our planet.

SPECIES PROFILES

The Tasmanian devil is an iconic ecosystem engineer instrumental in rebuilding Australia's lost ecosystems. The saola is an elusive myth-like animal and flagship for the Annamite Mountains, also known as the "Asian Unicorn." The critically endangered northern white-cheeked gibbon plays an important role dispersing seeds in Vietnam and Laos.

> **In order to reverse the climate crisis and ecosystem collapse, we need to focus on a 'technology' that took billions of years to refine, that is free, and that sustains us every single day: nature, in its most wild form.**
>
> Wes Sechrest, chief scientist and CEO of Re:wild

EASTERN FORESTS, AUSTRALIA

A global biodiversity hotspot that we are working to rewild one species at a time.

THE FUTURE

Healthy, thriving ecosystems in Australia and the Annamites with a full complement of native wildlife will show that we can rewild some of the most biodiverse and irreplaceable places on Earth!

PROJECT IN ACTION

In Australia we work with local partners Aussie Ark to reintroduce Tasmanian devils into predator-free areas, and to monitor their success, building on years of a successful conservation breeding program. In the Annamites we work with WWF Vietnam, Bach Ma National Park, and Wroclaw Zoo. Communities around the project sites and conservation breeding centers benefit from direct employment and enhanced tourism potential.

FIND OUT MORE
> FOLLOW REWILD ON SOCIAL MEDIA TO STAY UP TO DATE WITH OUR ONGOING CONSERVATION WORK.

THE CLOUD FOREST

DEVELOPED WITH
CALLIE BROADDUS
WRITTEN BY
MARGUERITE BENNETT
ART & COLORS BY
MAIA KOBABE
LETTERING BY
BERNARDO BRICE

THIS IS OUR HOME, THE BEAUTIFUL CHOCÓ CLOUD FOREST OF ECUADOR.

AND THE HUMANS MAKE IT SMALLER BY THE DAY.

THEY TAKE OUR TREES FOR CATTLE.

COME ON, I THINK THERE ARE A FEW MOUTHFULS OF GRASS OVER THERE--

HEY, I'M SLITHERIN' HERE!

THERE GOES THE NEIGHBORHOOD--

THEY TAKE OUR MOUNTAINS FOR GOLD.

WAITER, THERE'S SOUP ON MY FLY!

THEY TAKE OUR FOOD WITH PESTICIDES.

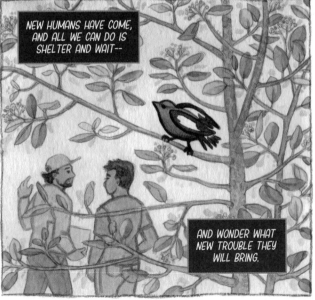

NEW HUMANS HAVE COME, AND ALL WE CAN DO IS SHELTER AND WAIT--

AND WONDER WHAT NEW TROUBLE THEY WILL BRING.

BUT INSTEAD...THEY MEAN US NO HARM.

THEY HAVE COME TO PROTECT US. THEY'VE COME TO LEARN FROM US.

THEY DISCOVER, DOCUMENT, AND LET US GO.

THEY SAY WE ARE RARE BEYOND RARE. THAT ONLY WITHIN THIS EVER-DWINDLING CLOUD FOREST ARE WE FOUND.

THAT SOME OF US WERE THOUGHT LOST, GONE FOREVER FROM THE EARTH, AND ARE REBORN, REDISCOVERED BY THESE HUMANS WHO COME TO HELP.

FOR SO LONG, WE HAVE BEEN HIDDEN--HAVE BEEN HIDING, AND SCARED, AND SILENT.

BUT NOW THAT YOU KNOW WE ARE HERE...

FINALLY, I HOPE WE CAN UNDERSTAND ONE ANOTHER.

THANK YOU! THANK YOU! THANK YOU...

RESERVA
THE YOUTH LAND TRUST

THE MONEY WE RAISE IS HELPING:

A FUTURE FOR THE CHOCÓ

The Chocó is one of the most ecologically unique places on Earth, but rampant deforestation for ranching, agriculture, and extractive industries like gold mining and commercial logging are quickly reducing this critically biodiverse zone to a fraction of its original size.

WHY IS THE PROJECT SO IMPORTANT?

While scientists race to study this area's endangered, new-to-science, and endemic species—that live here and nowhere else—conservation groups are working together to build a network of strategic protected areas. They are purchasing plots of intact habitat that might otherwise be sold for commercial development and employing local and Indigenous people as forest guardians.

After establishing an entirely youth-funded nature reserve here in 2021 in partnership with Rainforest Trust and Fundación EcoMinga, Reserva is again championing a creative youth-led effort to protect what remains of this irreplaceable forest by matching letters from youth with actual funds for conservation.

This funding will support the purchase and protection of Ecuadorian Chocó cloud forest, securing habitat for the critically endangered brown-headed spider monkey, black-and-chestnut eagle, iconic species like the puma and spectacled bear, and thousands of other species—empowering young people along the way.

SPECIES PROFILES

The intricately patterned Rio Faisanes stubfoot toad is one of the most endangered amphibians in Ecuador, relying on the expansion of Dracula Reserve for its survival. The Brown-headed spider monkey is one of the top twenty-five most endangered primates in the world and one of the three species of monkey on this site. The Chocó is home to more than fifty endemic bird species, like this multicolored plate-billed mountain toucan.

> " *The first step to stopping extinction is halting the loss of wild habitat. We have to stop the bleeding. Literally.* "

Callie Broaddus, founder & executive director, Reserva: The Youth Land Trust

DRACULA YOUTH RESERVE, ECUADOR

The current edge of Dracula Youth Reserve is called Peñas Blancas (white rocks), situated in a conservation corridor established over eight years of international collaboration.

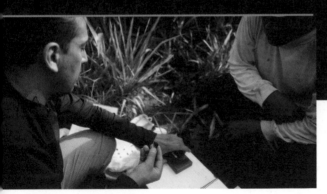

THE FUTURE

The Ecuadorian Chocó is uniquely understudied, with nearly every expedition unearthing a new-to-science frog, mouse, or orchid. By empowering youth to have a hand in protecting this ecosystem both from afar and through local engagement, this project is also protecting the future of discovery for a generation of children and young scientists growing up with dwindling wild places to explore.

FIND OUT MORE
> CONTRIBUTE TO OUR 1 MILLION LETTERS #FORNATURE CAMPAIGN.
> FOLLOW @RESERVAYLT ON SOCIAL MEDIA TO SEE UPDATES ON OUR YOUTH-LED CONSERVATION EFFORTS!

PROJECT IN ACTION

Funding for this project covers the cost of purchasing, protecting, and understanding this critically biodiverse landscape, including the expeditions necessary to monitor wildlife and salaries for local and Indigenous staff who are hired to protect these fragile ecosystems. Land will be owned and managed by Ecuadorian NGO Fundación EcoMinga.

...AND THERE'S EVEN MORE OF US AT

THE "WILD PLACE"?

DEVELOPED WITH
REBECCA WRIGLEY

WRITTEN BY
RIK WORTH

ART & LETTERING BY
JORDAN COLLVER

COLORS BY
OWEN WATTS

I'M TELLING YOU, IT'S TRUE! MORE ANIMALS, MORE PLANTS.

A WHOLE SOCIETY!

groan

grumble

BUT...

...HOW?

THE **BUILDERS** BROUGHT THE WILD BACK. THEY CHANGED THE RIVERS, HEALED THE SOIL.

EVEN THE SUMMERS ARE COOLER.

PAH! WE'VE BEEN MARCHING FOR DAYS. WE'RE STARVING. WE SHOULD GO BACK HO--

BZZZ ZZZZZZZ

ZZZZZZZZZZ ZZZ

BUZZ OFF!

BACK TO THE **GREEN DESERT?** THERE'S NOTHING THERE FOR US ANYMORE.

I BARELY MADE IT THROUGH LAST WINTER...

...and I was one of the lucky ones.

WELL IT MAY NOT BE MUCH...

...BUT AT LEAST IT AIN'T JUST **A MYTH.** WE'RE OUTTA HERE!

YOU WANNA BELIEVE IN FAIRY TALES, KID?

YOU'LL DIE LOOKIN' FOR A PLACE THAT DON'T EXIST **NO MORE.**

WHAT'S THE PROBLEM?

IN MANY PLACES ACROSS THE WORLD, PEOPLE ARE UNAWARE OF WHAT **THE WILD** SHOULD LOOK LIKE...

FOR EXAMPLE, MOST OF BRITAIN'S LAND HAS BEEN CULTIVATED AND SHAPED BY HUMANS TO SERVE OUR PURPOSES BUT IS **BEREFT OF LIFE!**

WILDLIFE IS CURRENTLY **DISCONNECTED**, SURVIVING IN SMALL FRAGMENTS OF LAND.

WE NEED TO EXPAND, RESTORE AND **JOIN UP** WILD PLACES SO THAT SPECIES CAN **MOVE SAFELY** -- OR WE'LL BE FACING MORE MASS EXTINCTIONS.

LET NATURE DO ITS THING!

"REWILDING" AIMS TO RESTORE ECOSYSTEMS TO THE POINT WHERE NATURE CAN TAKE CARE OF ITSELF.

WHEN IT DOES, EVERYBODY WINS!

WOODLANDS STAND STRONGER. WETLANDS THRIVE. SEAS FLOURISH. PEOPLE PROSPER.

THE WILD IS GOOD FOR PEOPLE TOO...

WE SHOULDN'T NEED TO TRAVEL TO ANOTHER COUNTRY TO BENEFIT FROM WILD PLACES!

WITH REWILDING, WE CAN CREATE NEW **NATURE-BASED ECONOMIES** AND **BEAUTIFUL EXPERIENCES** WITHIN WALKING DISTANCE OF EVERYONE'S HOMES.

FROM LEAVING PARTS OF YOUR GARDEN TO GROW WILD, TO REWILDING **30%** OF THE PLANET -- REWILDING CAN WORK **AT ALL SCALES** IN A WAY UNRIVALLED BY ANY OTHER ACTION.

WE CAN DO IT. WE KNOW HOW. WE JUST NEED TO RAISE OUR VOICES AND CALL FOR CHANGE!

...NO.

THERE ARE *DEER* IN THE WOODS. IS *THEIR* BLOOD NOT AS HOT? THEIR STRUGGLE NOT AS FINE? CULL THEM *WELL* AND THE FORESTS SHALL FLOURISH.

RF.

DEER ARE *HARD.* FLEET LEAPERS. SWIFT OF HORN AND WARY.

WE WILL HAVE THE *SOFT* MEAT. THE SOFT MEAT IS *EASY.*

...NO.

THE SOFT MEAT IS *MINE.*

THE SOFT MEAT IS *DEATH.*

A *THREAT.* FOOLISH.

HM. *DIVIDE,* THEN. *SURROUND.* MY TEETH DO NOT *NEED* TO FIND YOU ALL.

HERE IS MY PROMISE:

I WILL TEAR OUT *ONE* THROAT BEFORE YOU OVERWHELM ME.

THE BIGGEST, PERHAPS. *OR* THE LITTLEST. IT DOESN'T MATTER.

THE PACK *SHRINKS.* THE SCENTS FADE. THE NIGHT LOSES A VOICE.

IS THE SOFT MEAT WORTH THAT?

WHAT DO *YOU* KNOW OF *PACKS*, LONESOME THING?!

YOU ARE *MISTAKEN*, DOG. THE SOFT MEAT IS THE *GIFT* OF THE TALL WALKERS. THEY ARE OUR *FRIENDS.*

"THERE HAS BEEN NO PACK HERE IN A HUNDRED MOONS, BUT WE HAVE *SEEN* THE SIGNS. WE HAVE FOUND THE *BONES.*

"THIS IS *WOLF* LAND. THE TALL WALKERS *KNOW* IT. IT WAS *THEY* WHO MOVED US TO THESE HILLS--DO YOU NOT SEE THAT THEY *WANT* US TO FLOURISH?

"DOES IT NOT FOLLOW THAT THEY *WANT* US TO HAVE THE *SOFT MEAT?*"

IT IS *YOU* WHO ARE MISTAKEN. THE TALL WALKERS ARE NOT *ALIKE.*

I KNOW THEM. THEY *RAISED* ME. THEY *FEED* ME.

HUH. PERHAPS *YOU* ARE SOFT MEAT, TOO...

THEN *COME!* TEST MY *TEETH* IF YOU THINK ME FEEBLE. LET US *BOTH DIE!* LET YOUR PACK *STEAL* THE SOFT MEAT AND *FEAST* WITHOUT YOU!

BUT KNOW THIS. NEXT TIME THEY COME?

"THUNDER. BLOOD.

"METAL *JAWS* IN THE EARTH AND *POISON* IN THEIR BELLIES."

Dark Souls

Tree Hugger

"THE ABOMINABLE CHARLES CHRISTOPHER" COMIC STRIPS BY **KARL KERSCHL**

£1,000,000
2,500 hectres of
land rewilded.

£500,000
1,250 hectres of
land rewilded.

£100,000
250 hectres of
land rewilded.

£10,000
25 hectres of
land rewilded.

Rewilding
Europe®

THE MONEY WE RAISE IS HELPING:

MAKE EUROPE A WILDER PLACE

Many ecosystems, the basis of our natural wealth, are broken. But there is a way to fix it. It's called rewilding, and it's about giving nature the space to restore itself. Massive restoration of nature through rewilding will support wildlife comeback, help overcome the climate and biodiversity emergencies, and will improve our quality of life.

WHY IS THE PROJECT SO IMPORTANT?

Rewilding ecosystems across Europe is one of the best ways of tackling our current climate and biodiversity emergencies. It does not only benefit wild nature, but it also enhances the wide range of benefits that such nature gives all Europeans—from clean air and water, carbon sequestration and fertile soil, right through to flood protection, climate change resilience, and enhanced health and well-being.

We can give nature a helping hand to heal by creating the right conditions—by removing dams that are no longer needed from rivers, by allowing natural forest regeneration, and by reintroducing species that have disappeared. Then we should step back and trust nature to manage itself.

This funding will allow important wildlife species to come back, like the Iberian lynx and the Griffon vulture. These species play a critically important role and are part of the restoration of entire ecosystems.

SPECIES PROFILES

After years of decline, the European populations of some wildlife species are increasing. Such species include the lynx, vultures, and wild horses. They each play a critically important ecological role in a healthy ecosystem, yet numbers are still low. Rewilding will accelerate their recovery, boost biodiversity, and restore the important functions they play in driving many ecological processes.

> **" We need to do more than simply protect the nature we have left. We need to restore nature by rewilding large areas across the world. "**

Frans Schepers, managing director and co-founder of Rewilding Europe

CARPATHIAN MOUNTAINS, ROMANIA

One of the rewilding areas.
A wilderness arc at the heart
of Europe.

THE FUTURE

In the future Europe is a wilder place, with much more space for wild nature, wildlife, and natural processes shaping the landscapes. Wild nature has become a fundamental part of Europe's heritages and is an essential element in a modern, prosperous, and healthy society, creating new sources of income and pride amongst European citizens.

FIND OUT MORE
> JOIN THE REWILDING MOVEMENT! FOLLOW REWILDING EUROPE ON SOCIAL MEDIA AND SUBSCRIBE TO OUR NEWSLETTER AND STAY UPDATED ON THE LATEST REWILDING NEWS.

PROJECT IN ACTION

Rewilding is about the mass restoration of ecosystems, supporting wildlife comeback, and creating space where nature can govern itself without human intervention. Large areas of wild nature and abundant wildlife across our continent are created as inspirational showcases, benefitting both nature and people by boosting local economies where alternatives are scarce.

THE LONG VIEW

DEVELOPED WITH
SIR CHARLIE BURRELL, ISSY TREE, RUSS CARRINGTON AND REBECCA WRIGLEY

WRITTEN BY
GEORGE MANN

ART BY
TAZIO BETTIN

COLORS BY
NICOLA RIGHI

INDUSTRIAL AGRICULTURE
INDUSTRIAL UK FARMING
AND POST WAR RECOVERY
FOR POST WAR RECOVERY

When it started snowing ash in Sydney it was one of the worst moments of my life...

But for all my pain and anxiety it was nothing compared to the suffering of those who were there...

After all the years of warnings... it felt like we had finally run out of time...

The Australian Wildfires undeniably proved our world is on the brink.

It felt like we were inheriting a flat-lining future.

BETTER
THE
DEVIL

DACRE MONTGOMERY AND RE:WILD

WRITTEN BY
SARAH FLORENCE LORD

IAN STOPFORTH
LETTERING BY
PAUL GOODENOUGH

Australia has the worst mammal extinction in the world — we are just adding ourselves to the list.

We need to reverse the decline. We need to rebuild the natural defences that were here **before**.

Wildfire's start when there's a **build up** of flammable forest material.

But there's an animal that can help **change** that...

Help us Bring the Devil Back and stop the decline

The Tasmanian Devil has been absent from mainland Australia for 3,000 years. But they hold the key to keeping our forests clear of brush and re-establishing our precious ecosystem.

Thank you for your love and support for our mission. From Dacre, Sarah, Ian and Re:wild

THEY KEEP ASKING ME WHEN I'M GOING TO SLOW DOWN.

NO CHAMPIONSHIP TO MY NAME. NEVER WILL BE NOW. LONG ACCEPTED THAT.

BUT THEY STILL DON'T GET IT.

Final lap for 51-year-old racer?

OH, I SEE THE SOCIAL MEDIA, TOO. *"TOO OLD FASHIONED"?* MAYBE.

BUT THIS ISN'T THE SORT OF FAMILIARITY THAT BREEDS CONTEMPT. KINDA THE OPPOSITE.

75MPH

AND DON'T GET ME WRONG. PLAUDITS ARE NICE. NO MATTER HOW RARE.

BUT I'M LOOKING AT SOMETHING ELSE.

WHICH LEADS TO THE FOLLOW-UP QUESTION I ALWAYS GET:

"SO... WHY?"

BECAUSE IT'S NEVER JUST ABOUT THE RACE WE SEE.

IT'S A MISCONCEPTION THAT PROFESSIONAL DRIVERS HAVE TUNNEL VISION.

HEY, YOU'D BE SURPRISED AT HOW MANY OTHER THINGS WE CAN FOCUS ON. *(YES, EVEN THE "OLDER" DRIVERS.)*

IT'S THAT SAME FOCUS THAT SEES THESE POOR CREATURES TRY TO RETURN WITHIN 150 METERS OF WHERE THEY WERE BORN, TO LAY NEW EGGS.

BUT THE RISING SEA LEVELS PREVENT THAT.

CAN YOU IMAGINE TRYING TO COME BACK TO YOUR OLD FAMILY HOUSE, ONLY TO FIND A GIANT SAND CLIFF IN FRONT OF IT?

THE TURTLES DON'T KNOW HOW TO GET PAST THAT. THEY SIMPLY JUST WANT TO GET HOME.

MOST BREAK THEIR NECKS FROM THE FALL.

AND THAT'S JUST ONE ANSWER AS TO *"WHY."*

THERE'RE MANY MORE.

WE JUST NEED TO GO THAT LITTLE BIT FASTER.

THEY KEEP ASKING ME WHEN I'M GOING TO SLOW DOWN.

VRRR--

VRRRRRMMMM

VRRRMMH

ACCELERATION

DEVELOPED WITH	WRITTEN BY
ALEJANDRO AGAG AND EXTREME E	COREY BROTHERSON
ART & COLORS BY	LETTERING BY
KENNEDY GARZA	LUCAS GATTONI

...AND *RIGHT NOW* WE'RE HARD AT WORK INTRODUCING *BISON* TO REWILDED *WOODLANDS* AND BRINGING BACK *BUTTERFLIES* AND *FARMLAND BIRDS.*

WE *CAN* DO IT. WE *KNOW HOW,* WE JUST NEED THE WILL TO MAKE IT HAPPEN.

THE WILL TO TRANSFORM OUR NATION INTO A PLACE WHERE WILD SPACES ARE AVAILABLE TO ALL, NOT JUST THE PRIVILEGED...

...WHERE OUR TOWNS AND CITIES ARE ALIVE WITH THE MUSIC OF WILDLIFE...

THE MONEY WE RAISE IS HELPING:

BRING BEAVERS BACK

The UK is one of the most nature-depleted places in the world, which is why The Wildlife Trusts have a big ambition to restore at least 30% of land and sea for nature by 2030. And beavers are key to helping us do just that! With their super engineering abilities, they inject new life into wild places, ensuring a brighter future for our wetlands and the wildlife and people that live in and around them.

WHY IS THE PROJECT SO IMPORTANT?

The next ten years will be critical in determining what kind of world we live in. We need nature for our health and well-being, food production, and to tackle the climate emergency.

It is not enough to slow the loss of wild places and the species that depend on them—we urgently need to reverse the decline and put nature into recovery. Beavers create a fantastic range of wetland habitats that provide homes for other wildlife and help address the climate emergency by locking up carbon. Not only that, the channels, dams, and wetlands that beavers engineer hold back water and release it more slowly after heavy rain, helping to reduce flooding, currently on the increase due to climate change. But these brilliant natural engineers have long been missing from Britain's landscapes, having been hunted to extinction in the 16th century. The loss of beavers led to the disappearance of the magical mosaic of lakes, meres, and boggy places that they created.

We're turning that around, and with your help, beavers will be back where they belong, creating wilder spaces that benefit us all.

SPECIES PROFILES

Kingfishers need our help because they are at risk from habitat degradation and pollution. These striking birds depend on healthy wetlands. Beavers were driven to extinction in Britain 400 years ago but are starting to return thanks to Wildlife Trust efforts. Ospreys are making a remarkable comeback. Once lost through persecution, these awe-inspiring birds fly 5,000 km back to the UK every summer to raise their chicks in our wetlands.

> **" The next ten years must be a time of renewal, of rewilding our lives, of green recovery. "**
>
> Craig Bennett, chief executive, The Wildlife Trusts

WETLANDS, UNITED KINGDOM

UK wetlands can be a perfect home to beavers and help store carbon, too.

THE FUTURE

We are creating a wilder future, where nature is abundant everywhere—in our towns, cities, and countryside. With more space for nature, rare wildlife will no longer cling on in isolated pockets on the brink of disappearing altogether, but thrive. Locally extinct species such as beavers have helped us bring back healthy, functioning ecosystems that sustain us and our planet. Together, with your help and support, we will get nature working again.

FIND OUT MORE

> FOLLOW THE WILDLIFE TRUSTS, AND OUR 30 BY 30 CAMPAIGN TO FIND OUT WHAT WE'RE DOING, AND HOW YOU CAN HELP.
> WILDLIFETRUSTS.ORG/30-30-30

PROJECT IN ACTION

Right now, The Wildlife Trusts are working with communities to secure and manage more land for nature, rewild whole landscapes, bring back lost species such as beavers, and create the green jobs of the future. We are working in partnership with local communities to reintroduce families of beavers across the UK, studying their impact on their surroundings, mapping the best possible locations, and campaigning to secure their long-term future.

PART OF THE REASON FOR PEOPLES' HESITATION TO MAKE CHANGES THAT BENEFIT THE ENVIRONMENT IS DUE TO THE SCALE THEY THINK IS REQUIRED.

REGENERATIONAL CHANGE

IT'S EASY TO THINK "IT'S A GLOBAL MESS--ENVIRONMENTAL ISSUES ABOUND ALL OVER THE WORLD, SO WHAT DIFFERENCE CAN *ONE PERSON* MAKE?"

DEVELOPED WITH
GABE BROWN
WRITTEN BY
CHRIS RYALL
ART BY
MIKE COLLINS
COLORS BY
SEBASTIAN CHENG & CANDICE HAN
LETTERING BY
JIM CAMPBELL
WITH THANKS TO
ARIZONA MUSE

OR "IT'S *TOO MUCH*--CLEAR AIR, CLEAN WATER, PESTICIDES AND FACTORY FARMING AND DESERTIFICATION OF OUR SOIL, THERE'RE *SO MANY PROBLEMS...*

"...AND CLIMATE CHANGE IS SUCH A COMPLICATED PROBLEM THAT NOTHING I DO MYSELF WILL MAKE ENOUGH OF A DIFFERENCE.

"IT'S NOT THAT DIRE. ENVIRONMENTAL DISASTERS LIKE THE DUST BOWL HAPPENED ALMOST 100 YEARS AGO AND WE'RE STILL GOING."

WHICH ISN'T TRUE. AND WE'RE NOT ONLY STILL REPLICATING THE PROBLEMS THAT CREATED SUCH DISASTERS AS THE DUST BOWL, WE'RE ACCELERATING THEM. MOST DROUGHTS ARE NOT NATURAL--THEY'RE MAN-MADE.

INDUSTRIAL TILLING, A LACK OF GROWING PLANTS AND BAD DECISIONS HAVE LED US TO WHERE WE ARE--TO A PRECIPICE MADE OF CRUMBLING, NUTRIENT-STARVED DIRT... *FOR NOW.*

BUT THE SOLUTION IS AS INTERCONNECTED AS THE WORLD ITSELF. SMALL MOVES **CAN** AND **DO** COMBINE TO MAKE BIG, POSITIVE CHANGE.

NUTRIENT-FREE DIRT WASN'T ALWAYS SO. AND IT DOESN'T NEED TO REMAIN BARREN... NOW WE HAVE THE ANSWER.

ONE THING THE PLANET DOES WELL WHEN GIVEN THE CHANCE IS REJUVENATE.

THROUGH A PROCESS CALLED **REGENERATIVE FARMING**, WE CAN TRANSFORM DIRT BACK INTO THE NUTRIENT-RICH, CARBON-ABSORBING SOIL IT ONCE WAS. WE CAN **PREVENT** ANOTHER DUST BOWL.*

*AS SEEN ON THE **KISS THE GROUND** DOCUMENTARY--ED.

REGENERATIVE AGRICULTURE HAS ALREADY BEEN USED TO RESTORE MILLIONS OF ACRES ACROSS THE WORLD...

...TURNING DESERT-LIKE LAND THAT HAD BEEN INTENSIVELY AND INDUSTRIALLY TILLED INTO INFERTILITY BACK TO THE PLANT-HEALTHY, ANIMAL-SUSTAINING SOIL IT ONCE WAS.

FARMERS WHO MAKE THIS KIND OF A CHANGE INCREASE THEIR FARM'S PROFITABILITY AND OUTPUT, AS WELL AS THE NUTRITIONAL CONTENT OF THEIR CROP YIELD.

BY PLANTING **MIXED COVER CROPS** AND GRAZING THESE WITH LIVESTOCK, FARMERS BUILD A CIRCULAR ECOSYSTEM WHERE ANIMALS FERTILIZE THE COVER CROPS WHILE GRAZING. THIS ENCOURAGES PLANTS TO DEVELOP LONGER ROOTS--WHICH **CAPTURES CARBON** RATHER THAN **RELEASING IT**...

...THIS REVITALIZATION DOES MORE THAN BENEFIT THE SOIL AND ITS CROPS: IT ALSO PROVIDES BOTH RESTORATIVE AND ECONOMIC BENEFITS TO THE SURROUNDING COMMUNITIES.

FARMERS CAN **RENEW** THE SOIL AND CREATE A MORE SUSTAINABLE ECO-SYSTEM. IT DOESN'T TAKE LONG FOR THE GROUND, AND THE LIVESTOCK THAT FEEDS OFF IT, TO SEE POSITIVE RESULTS.

IT'S SOMETHING REGENERATIVE FARMERS LIKE GABE BROWN HAVE PROVEN SUCCESSFUL AND HELPFUL. BUT IT'S NOT ONLY THE FARMERS WHO CAN AFFECT THIS KIND OF POSITIVE CHANGE.

FIRST, THE FOODS YOU BUY AND WHERE YOU BUY THEM CAN DEMONSTRATE TO THESE FARMERS THEIR EFFORTS ARE NOT JUST WORTHWHILE BUT **SUSTAINABLE** FOR THEM.

ALSO, ANY TREES YOU CAN PLANT COMPLEMENT THE MANY OTHER EFFORTS TO REDUCE CARBON IN THE ATMOSPHERE. IT DOESN'T TAKE MUCH, AND THE ENVIRONMENTAL RELIEF IT BRINGS IS EXPONENTIAL...**WORLD CHANGING.**

AND YOUR OWN GARDENS--LARGE OR SMALL, BACKYARD OR WINDOWSILL--CAN FOLLOW THESE SAME SIMPLE STEPS TO SOIL HEALTH.

6 PRINCIPLES

Of Soil Health

THE VEGETATION DIVERSITY LEADS TO GREATER BIODIVERSITY AND PROVIDES NUTRIENT-RICH SOIL WITH REAL MEANS TO WARD OFF PREDATORY PESTS.

REDUCED PESTS MEAN LESS DAMAGE TO THE CROPS AND REDUCED NEED FOR SOIL- AND CROP-DAMAGING PESTICIDES.

1
Know your context.
Our soil health practices are a reflection of ourselves and our stewardship of the land.

2
Do not disturb.
In nature, there is no mechanical or chemical disturbance.

3
Cover and build surface armor
to protect the soil's "skin."

4
Mix it up
with a diversity of plants, microbes, insects, wildlife, livestock. Mother Nature did not grow monocultures so why should we?

5
Keep living roots in the soil
as long as possible each year. Roots feed soil microorganisms, which feed our plants.

6
Grow healthy animals and soil together.
Grazing has been an essential component of all soils at one time or another.

brought to you by SOIL HEALTH ACADEMY

REGENERATIVE FARMING IS AS IMPORTANT AS IT IS EFFECTIVE. AND IT'S SOMETHING EVERYONE CAN HELP WITH AND PARTICIPATE IN, FARMER OR URBAN-DWELLER.

PLANTS AND TREES ARE EFFECTIVE AT PULLING CARBON FROM THE ATMOSPHERE AND PLACING IT INTO THE SOIL, WHICH IS EQUIPPED TO PROCESS IT AND HOLD IT.

FROM THERE, A HEALTHY, CARBON-RICH BED OF SOIL HELPS INCREASE THE QUALITY OF LIFE OF THE PLANET AND THE PEOPLE ON IT.

IT'S NOT COMPLICATED TO DO. ALL IT REQUIRES IS GETTING YOUR HANDS A BIT DIRTY AND LETTING THE SOIL DO THE REST.

i do what i can

i can whenever i can

whenever i can

A Fevered Mind and a Pot of Pee
a sad but true account from Lucy Lawless

I learned that one of the important things when planting is learning how to produce **biochar**.

It's basically charcoal from wood burnt at very high heat with little oxygen, then doused with water and "activated" by being soaked in nitrogen for three weeks.

You **can** use slurry for the nitrogen, but I didn't exactly have any.

There is one thing that can do the job nicely... **pee!** And I can make that allllll day... and I even have **some** control over the volume...

And I found this old beaten-up pot amongst the bushes. "That'll do," I thought.

So yeah, I've been living on the farm, **sorry, I should say "my home"** now... With no landline, no cell service and no wi-fi for **months**.

It doesn't feel very safe... so not really the best time to get a head cold, you might say...

So what do you do?
You remember why you do
these things, right?

"Why you'd risk your career
and leave Bel Air to buy a
farm to rewild?", they ask.

Well...because I can!
I'm lucky enough to have the
privilege of choice...and
once you know you can help,
how can you not?

So I do what I can,
whenever I can...
because too many people
have been screwed over
for far too long.

Here in New Zealand there's
this deal, converting sheep
farmers to dairy farmers...
and it's **impoverishing** our
farmers, our soil, our water
and our animals.

**They made more money in
the '90s!** Before they were
suckered into this intensive
farming BS.

Now, they're working
harder than ever to
make **less** money, and
they're inadvertently
destroying our country
and our environment too!

It's got to stop.

banj oak trees you plant them a whole economy
and you've got a whole economy

The other day, a young man named Nigel knocked on my door.

He said to me, "I see your trees are coming on"...

In my headcold-induced psychosis, I said something to the effect of:

"Can you believe what's going on?! They're planting these $*%#&@ pine forests everywhere and they make really $*%#&@ timber and after two or three times planting those trees the soil's bloody **useless!** **Banj Oak** trees...that's the answer! You plant them instead and you've got a whole **economy!** The animals love their acorns, the timber from it is super thick and it stores a $*%#&@ ton of carbon AND you can grow all sorts of stuff on their bases!"

Poor Nigel's response?!

"I'm umm...just here to set-up your wi-fi, Miss Lawless..."

This damned sickness seems never ending.

But I just keeping going. Planting. Peeing. Planting. Peeing...

And just when I think it will never end...

It does...just in time. I just needed to keep going.

Now if you'll excuse me, I have some more 'business' to attend to.

$%&@...where did I leave that pot?!

WRITTEN BY	ART BY	LETTERING BY
LUCY LAWLESS, PAUL GOODENOUGH & TYLER JENNES	DAVID MACK	PAUL GOODENOUGH

GROW YOUR OWN, SAVE THE WORLD

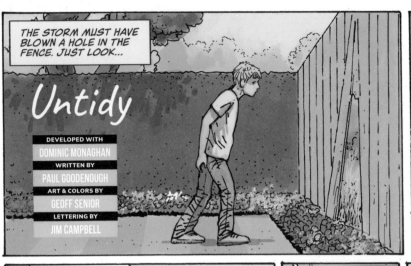

THE STORM MUST HAVE BLOWN A HOLE IN THE FENCE. JUST LOOK...

Untidy

DEVELOPED WITH
DOMINIC MONAGHAN
WRITTEN BY
PAUL GOODENOUGH
ART & COLORS BY
GEOFF SENIOR
LETTERING BY
JIM CAMPBELL

DAAAVIIIID!

YOU BEST NOT BE MESSING AROUND ON MY LAWN AGAIN. I'M BLOOMING WARNIN' YOU!

HOW MANY TIMES DO I HAVE TO *TELL YOU?*

MY GARDEN ISN'T FOR MESSING ABOUT IN! NOW GET IN HERE BEFO--

...DAD?

CALL AN AMBULANCE, DAVID!

QUICK!

AS THE AMBULANCE TOOK MY DAD AWAY, I COULD STILL HEAR HIM MUMBLING...

"GET THOSE... BLOODY DIRTY SHOES OFF MY FLOOR..."

I KNEW IF I WAITED FOR EVEN A SINGLE HEARTBEAT MY COURAGE'D BE GONE!

SO I SHUT MY EYES, HOPED MY DAD WAS ASLEEP AND--

--I STEPPED THROUGH.

I'D NEVER SEEN THE OIL FACTORY IN REAL LIFE. ONLY PICTURES. AND THEY DIDN'T LOOK ANYTHING LIKE THIS!

AND INSIDE THERE WAS A WHOLE OTHER WORLD.

ANTS, WOODLICE, MILLIPEDES...IS THAT FUNGAL HYPHAE?

NEMATODE WORMS, SPRINGTAILS, SILVERFISH...

CENTIPEDES, BEETLES AND GRUBS...

JEN!! WHERE'S THAT ⸸HACK HACK HACK⸸ WHERE'S THAT SON OF OURS?

SOLDIER BEETLE, LACEWING, PILL BUG...MOUSE SPIDER... DUNNO WHAT THAT ONE'S CALLED...

LOOK AT IT OUT THERE! I KNOW HE'S BRINGING THAT...MESS IN FROM THE FACTORY. I DUNNO WHY. IT'S HORRIBLE! BLOODY HORRIBLE...

IT'S JUST... DIFFERENT!

EXACTLY! DIFF'ERENT! I LIKE IT ALL THE SAME. CLEAN. PERFECT! THIS...MESS IS--

YOU HAVE A WORD WITH THAT BOY OR I ⸸HACK HACK HACK⸸ I WILL.

WHERE'S HE GOING THIS TIME, THAT LITTLE--

⸸COUGH⸸ ⸸COUGH⸸

WHEN I GET MY HANDS ON THAT KID I'M GOING TO-- ⸸COUGH⸸ ⸸COUGH⸸

PEST-BE-DEAD

...

PEST-BE-DEAD

YOU SEE...I WAS BROUGHT UP TO LIKE THINGS TIDY...AN' I HAD THIS PICTURE IN MY HEAD-- I KNEW EXACTLY WHAT I WANTED MY GARDEN TO LOOK LIKE.

AND THEN *YOU* WENT AND MESSED IT ALL UP!

AND SOMEHOW, THIS GARDEN OF... *OURS,* WENT FROM BEING THIS PERFECT *PICTURE*...INTO LIKE... A STORY OR A FILM OR SOMETHING...

...AND EVERY DAY WAS DIFFERENT, *EVERY DAY*...

...GAVE ME A REASON TO GET UP. WELL, ASIDE FROM SCREAMING AT YOU. I'VE NEVER BREATHED SO *WELL* IN ME LIFE!

COME ON THEN...LET'S HAVE A LOOK AT OUR NEW *GUESTS!*

"Rewilding is not about abandoning civilization but about enhancing it."
—George Monbiot

INSPIRE

AND EDUCATE

The planet is in crisis and the ability for positive change lies with us all. How we appreciate and interact with the natural world, and the myriad species that call it their home, is now mission-critical.

Every single one of us can play a part in creating a better future and, to inspire us each step of the way, we've brought together some of the most influential voices on the planet to share their thoughts, fears, hopes, and dreams — and tell stories to help us all think, engage, be empowered, and take action.

I Love You, Earth

I love you, earth, you are beautiful I love the way you are
I know I never said it to you
But I wanna say it now

I love you, I Love you I love you, earth
I love you, I love you I love you nOw

I loVe you, earth, you are beautiful
I love the way you shine
I love your valleys, I love your mornings In fact I love you Everyday

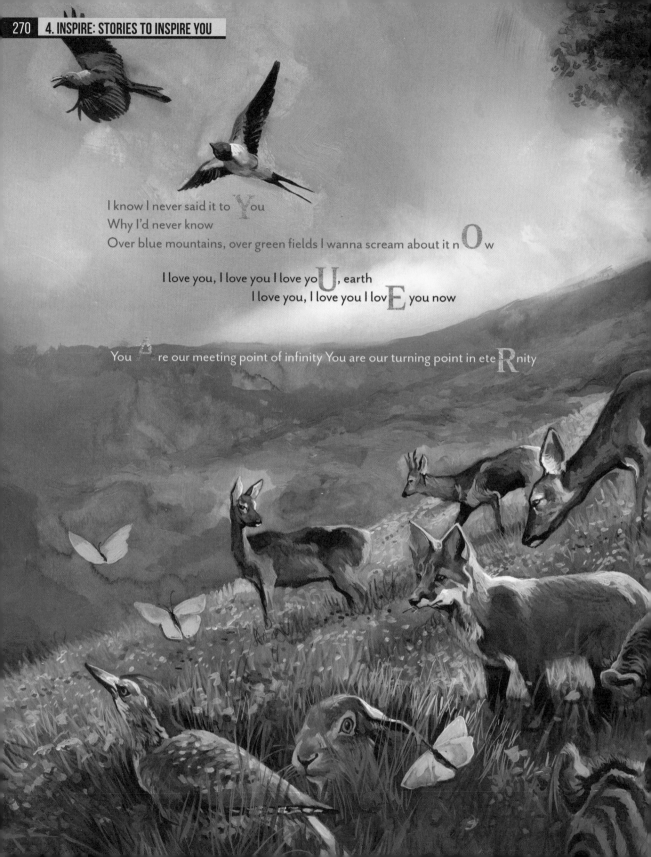

I know I never said it to You
Why I'd never know
Over blue mountains, over green fields I wanna scream about it nOw

I love you, I love you I love yoU, earth
I love you, I love you I lovE you now

You Are our meeting point of infinity You are our turning point in eteRnity

I love you, I love you (I love you, I love you) I love you, ear**T**h
I love you, I love you (I love you, I love you) I love you now
I love you, I love you (I love you, I love you) I love you, eart**H**
I love you, I love you (I love you, I love you) I love you now

YOKO ONO

IN PARTNERSHIP WITH
LETTERS TO THE EARTH

INSPIRED AND WRITTEN BY
YOKO ONO

ART & LETTERING BY
TIMO WUERTZ

Timo Wuerz 2021

USE YOUR VOICE

Dear Parliamentarians,

I have been a nurse for forty years;
I have worked for the last ten with people with dementia.
Dementia is no respecter of status, wealth, class, or prestige.
I have nursed doctors, lorry drivers, and paedophiles.
I accord them all the same human dignity and respect;
I give them appropriate care regardless of who they are and how they have
lived their lives.

I have learned to communicate with those whom dementia has
robbed of their ability to speak coherently;
I have learned to communicate with those who are mute,
literally having no voice.
You have a voice, and you have the status and power
to use your voices to represent those of us with none.

My five-month-old grandson does not yet have words; he communicates his
joy at life in myriad ways.
He laughs, he squeals, his smile beams like a beacon on a stormy day.
His joy is palpable; he wants to experience life in all its beauty and richness.
But if climate change continues as predicted by the IPCC
what will be his future?
And what of the future for your children and grandchildren?

Please, on behalf of all of those with no voice,
use yours to bring change, so we may all have a future.

Yours faithfully,
Marian Greaves RGN/Mother/Grandmother

Illustration by Dan Bradbury
In partnership with Letters To The Earth

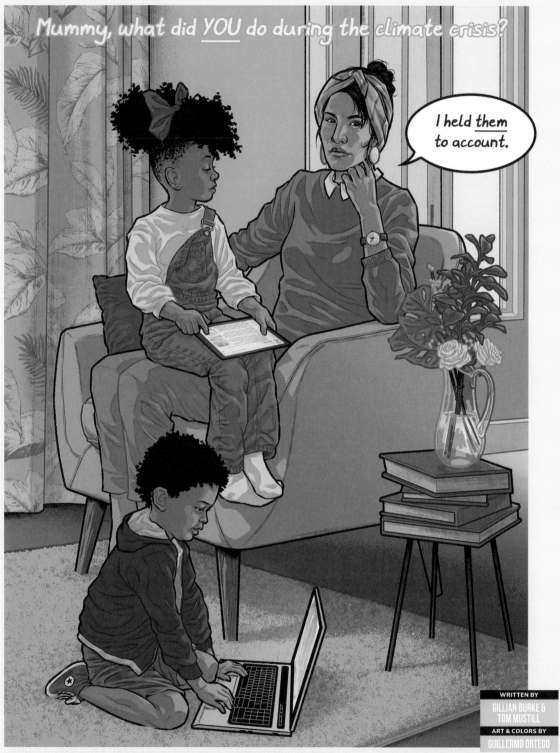

Just **3** companies emit **3** times more carbon than all UK households combined.
You're doing your bit. It's time for them to do theirs.

DR. GAIL BRADBROOK

Interview by John Wagner, Art by Abdulkareem Baba Aminu

WHY DID YOU DECIDE TO CREATE XR?
I'd been thinking about mass civil disobedience for years, trying to find people who felt the same because I didn't think things would change significantly without some form of dramatic action. In 2016 things fell into place when I finally got together with the right people.

HOW DID YOU SET ABOUT IT?
We did lots of research and took training in how to build social movements. We developed a talk and training aid and every time someone "liked" our Facebook page we contacted them to ask if they would organize a local talk. We already had a base, building from 2014–2018 through work I did with Compassionate Revolution and then together with a group we called Rising Up. We tried lots of small actions. It took us 25 iterations to think of the name Extinction Rebellion and some of us nearly fell out over it!

WHAT IS YOUR ATTITUDE TO THE DISRUPTION XR CAUSES?
On the one hand building a garden bridge in Waterloo and parking a boat in Oxford Circus, setting up a community at Marble Arch, they were glory days of togetherness and possibility, of saying "screw you" to a system that is killing life on Earth.

We fully understand that we can mess up people's days, especially if they are trying to get to see a loved one or deal with another important matter, and that's upsetting. It doesn't feel good inconveniencing people, stopping them going about their daily business, having them caught up in our actions. We know they can be indiscriminate in their targeting.

We do make some people angry, but my experience is many are resigned and accept the necessity of what we're doing. Often they thank us.

WHAT ARE YOUR MAIN AIMS RIGHT NOW?
For myself and the Money Rebellion team I am working with—to point out that we have failed to tackle this crisis because we have a political economy with destruction baked in.

We want to create a global citizens' assembly to help rewire humanity and challenge the fairly hidden power holding

bodies, like those that set international tax rules, or are wedded to economic growth. Above all we want to keep up the pressure on our governments. COP 26 is a good place to get our point across.

HOW DO YOU FEEL THE MOVEMENT SPREAD?
Because we had clear demands, tactics, a theory of change and principles and values—it was relatively easy to get involved and there was a zeitgeist, a wave that this built from, from the work of others: the IPCC report, Deep Adaptation (a social movement developed by Jem Bendell), Greta Thunberg, David Attenborough, the Sunrise Movement, etc.

DO YOU BELIEVE YOU CAN SUCCEED?
We can't—we have already failed. Climate tipping points are being breached now, there's no carbon budget left. We are managing a decline and a disaster that will kill millions, probably billions. We are living through the time when the biggest crimes against humanity are being committed.

Whatever success we have will be in living well, with integrity, and in working together to bring as much mitigation as we can to the climate disaster, in saving as much of our world as we can. It feels like we're hanging on to the possibility of a miracle—a great awakening and the best of humanity at last focusing on healing the damage we have done. It will require a global effort on a scale that's hard to imagine.

IF YOU COULD CHANGE ONE THING, WHAT WOULD IT BE?
That those with the most access to power in the world would wake up, collaborate and let go of the attachments they have to power and money, and go on a massive adventure of reimagining what is possible. I would like to see people like Rupert Murdoch changing their ways, to see billionaires using their money to fund the transition, to see the rapid demise of the fossil fuel industry.

And for people, all people to feel inspired to live well, with purpose and actions... Life wants us to live... It's a joyful thing to do, but you have to be willing to be transformed away from grief and to see your own power as the bright light that it is, to face fear and never give up, to find others like you and join forces.

ClimateTBD

WRITTEN AND DRAWN BY
ROSEMARY MOSCO

The people gathered for the time-honored ceremony
to welcome this precious newborn into their community.

And after all the words of gratitude for the seen and unseen
beings that made life so worth living had been spoken,
a hush fell upon them.

Slowly, the elder raised their clear eyes from the fire, swept
back their long hair, and from beneath smile lines
etched in shadow, spoke:

It is time for each of us to be reminded of the story that once was forgotten, and shall not be again, for it is a truth that has held our village through these past centuries and allowed us to thrive.

For it is said that back then, a great dread had taken hold... It seemed, they say, that all would surely be lost—and yet, because of this simple fire, there was a remembering of what long-distant cultures the world over had always known before the dread began.

This is how it was told to me:

The grandmothers noticed there was a need for the village council to be held in the light of a force greater than their own individual desires.

It is said that they sought guidance from the spirits of the directions, of the plants, and of the animals. They consulted with their ancestors, with the unborn generations and with the spirits of the land.

It is said that the spirit of fire offered itself in service. And so it was that a grandmother kindled a little fire and placed that flame at the centre of the council and had each one present make this pledge to that fire.

No decision, no thought, no action of any kind will emanate from this council unless it holds the good of the children of all beings, of this generation and seven generations hence, at its core.

And it is said that the making of this one simple pledge, held clean and pure by the transformative power of fire, marked the turning point, bringing life back to the people—and to all beings.

It is incumbent upon each of us to remember, in all that we do, to embody this pledge—to tend this fire by living our lives in honor of the children, and in this way, we too will become good ancestors.

AND SO, WITH THESE WORDS, I WELCOME YOU, PRECIOUS CHILD INTO THIS WORLD.

The Children's Fire, from those who would call us their ancestors.

Written by David Smart Knight and Jerome Flynn. Art by William Simpson.
In honor of the wisdom of our Indigenous Brothers and Sisters.

www.childrensfire.earth

REWILD FOR VICTORY

CONCEPT BY
TOM MUSTILL

POSTER DESIGNED BY
MAGGIE BEHLING

Future Archaeologist

ELIZABETH FINLEY BROADDUS WAS BORN MARCH 12TH, 1996.

FINLEY'S STORY

DEVELOPED WITH
CALLIE AND FINLEY BROADDUS

WRITTEN & DRAWN BY
PHILIP SEVY

CONCERNED ABOUT CLIMATE CHANGE, SHE WOULD SPEND THE MAJORITY OF HER TIME TALKING TO HER NEIGHBORS AND PEOPLE AROUND HER ABOUT THE IMPORTANCE OF MAKING AN IMPACT ON THE ENVIRONMENT.

SHE COULD BE FOUND AFTER SCHOOL PICKING UP TRASH ON THE SIDE OF THE ROAD.

ON CHRISTMAS DAY, 2013, SHE WAS DIAGNOSED WITH CHOLANGIOCARCINOMA, AN AGGRESSIVE AND TERMINAL CANCER.

SHE WOULD ONLY LIVE FIVE MORE MONTHS.

BUT IN THOSE FIVE MONTHS, SHE CHANGED THE WORLD.

WHILE IN THE HOSPITAL, SHE STARTED RECEIVING LOTS OF STUFFED ANIMALS AND FLOWER BOUQUETS.

SHE KNEW THAT GIFTS LIKE THESE WERE ONLY CAUSING MORE PROBLEMS FOR THE ENVIRONMENT, SO SHE ASKED THAT PEOPLE PLANT A TREE AND SEND HER A PICTURE OF IT INSTEAD.

WHEN PICTURES CAME POURING IN FROM ALL OVER THE WORLD, SHE KNEW THAT SHE COULD USE HER POSITION TO INSPIRE PEOPLE TO DO MORE.

WITH HER FAMILY, SHE STARTED THE "FINLEY'S GREEN LEAP FORWARD" FUND WITH A GOAL TO RAISE $18,000 BY HER 18TH BIRTHDAY-- A MERE THREE WEEKS AWAY.

ON HER BIRTHDAY, HER FAMILY PRESENTED HER A CHECK FOR THE FULL AMOUNT RAISED ALONG WITH A LIST OF ALL 432 DONORS.

THE CHECK WAS FOR OVER $70,000.

DURING HER MONTHS OF TREATMENT IN THE JOHNS HOPKINS PEDIATRIC ONCOLOGY WARD, FINLEY WOULD GET UP AND WALK AROUND THE UNIT.

ON MOST DAYS, SHE ONLY HAD THE ENERGY TO DO THIS ONCE.

AS SHE MADE HER ROUNDS, SHE WOULD STOP AT ALL THE EMPTY ROOMS AND TURN OFF THE LIGHTS TO CONSERVE ENERGY.

EVEN SEVEN YEARS AFTER HER PASSING, NURSES STILL COMMENT TO FINLEY'S FAMILY THAT THEY STOP IN EMPTY ROOMS AND TURN OFF THE LIGHTS BECAUSE OF THE IMPACT SHE MADE ON THEM.

YOU DON'T CHANGE THE WORLD BY GRAND GESTURES. YOU DO IT THROUGH INSPIRING OTHERS BY THE SMALL ACTIONS YOU TAKE.

MY NAME IS SARAH MINTRAM.

I'M MIXED RACE AND WORKING CLASS. FROM LIVERPOOL.

BABY ON BOARD

DEVELOPED WITH
SARAH MINTRAM
WRITTEN BY
ALEX SEGURA
ART BY
STEVEN AUSTIN
COLORS BY
PAUL GOODENOUGH
LETTERING BY
JIM CAMPBELL

Le Monde world, earth

I DON'T COME FROM A BACKGROUND OF ACTIVISM. WE WERE HAVING A VERY NICE LIFE. ENGLISH TEACHERS IN THE FRENCH COUNTRYSIDE. WE WENT VEGAN. WE WERE BOTH POLITICALLY MOTIVATED.

BUT WE FELT WE WEREN'T DOING ENOUGH.

CAN YOU BELIEVE THIS?

I HAD NO IDEA...

TELL THE TRUTH

We are facing an unprecedented global emergency. Life on Earth is in crisis: scientists agree we have entered a period of abrupt climate breakdown, and we are in the midst of a mass extinction of our own making.

Watch part 1 of the Extinction Rebellion talk (above) to see how we are heading for extinction.

WE BOTH FOUND EXTINCTION REBELLION AT THE SAME TIME. HE SAW A VIDEO ON YOUTUBE, I READ ABOUT IT IN 2018. IT WAS STRANGE WE BOTH SAW IT AT AROUND THE SAME TIME.

THE MESSAGE RESONATED WITH US.

WE HAD TO ACT TO SALVAGE WHAT WAS LEFT OF THIS WORLD.

WE ROSE THROUGH THE RANKS, SERVING "XR" ON AN INTERNATIONAL SCALE--WE GOT CONNECTED, AND IT BECAME A FULL-TIME GIG. FOURTEEN-HOUR DAYS.

MY HUSBAND BECAME A REGIONAL LIAISON. I FOCUSED ON AFRICA AND ASIA.

YOU LEARN FAST WITH XR. ABOUT THE RISKS. THE CULTURES, AND POLITICAL ISSUES EACH COUNTRY FACES WHEN IT COMES TO THE LOOMING CLIMATE DISASTER.

WILL YOU...?

YES, OF COURSE!

BUT WE HAD A LIFE, TOO. WE GOT ENGAGED. WE TALKED ABOUT CHILDREN, BUT YOUR WORK SEEPS INTO YOUR LIFE.

I...I JUST DON'T KNOW. I LOVE CHILDREN.

I WANT CHILDREN... BUT...

I KNOW. BUT HOW CAN WE...?

DID WE WANT TO BRING A CHILD INTO THIS WORLD? WE WERE TERRIFIED.

AS WE WENT ON, WE LEARNED ABOUT ACTIONS. ABOUT THE RHYTHM OF A PROTEST.

AND THE EXPECTED RISK.

YOU HAVE TO KNOW THE RISKS, AND KNOW YOUR STANCE.

I'M HERE AND I'M NOT MOVING! NO MATTER WHAT! ARREST ME IF YOU WANT!

GIVE THE CHILDREN A CHANCE

THE EXPERIENCE WAS NEW TO ME.

I'D SEEN POLICE, OF COURSE. BUT I'D NEVER BEEN ON THE OPPOSITE SIDE.

BACK OFF, ALL OF YOU. NOW.

THE KIDS TALK DID IT. A TURNING POINT, I GUESS. WE FIGURED IF YOU GOT ARRESTED AT A PROTEST, YOU'D GET A YEAR OR TWO SUSPENDED SENTENCE. THEN WE LEARNED IT'D BE CLOSER TO FIFTEEN **YEARS**.

IT WAS STRANGE TO THINK THAT EVEN THOUGH WE'D ONLY BEEN MARRIED FOR FIFTEEN MONTHS THAT HE COULD BE IN JAIL FOR MORE THAN TEN TIMES THAT.

BIRTH STRIKERS EXIST. I APPLAUD THEM. AND IF WE'RE SERIOUS ABOUT THE CAUSE AND WANT TO HAVE KIDS, WE NEED TO BE SERIOUS ABOUT OUR ACTIONS.

I COME FROM A STRONG IRISH BACKGROUND. FAMILY IS IMPORTANT. I KNEW I WANTED KIDS. REALLY WANTED. IT WAS A HARD CHOICE. BUT COULD I GIVE UP SOMETHING SO IMPORTANT?

WE FELT LIKE WE NEEDED TO WALK THE WALK.

SO WE DECIDED TO HAVE CHILDREN.

YES, YES...THIS IS THE RIGHT THING.

I'M SO HAPPY. LET'S MAKE THE WORLD BETTER FOR THIS BABY.

THANK YOU SO MUCH. YOU INSPIRE ME.

YOU MADE A CHOICE FOR ALL OF US.

...FOR SHOWING ME WE CAN BE MOTHERS AND ACTIVISTS...

SO MANY WOMEN REACHED OUT. FROM ALL OVER. SRI LANKA, EVEN. SAYING HOW MUCH THEY APPRECIATED THAT WE DID THIS.

THE STAKES HAVEN'T CHANGED. CLIMATE EMERGENCIES WILL MEAN WARS, FOOD SHORTAGES, CLASS DIVIDES, EXTINCTION EVENTS. IS IT FAIR TO BRING A CHILD INTO THIS WORLD?

CENSORED
BABY 'ON' BOARD

THE ANSWER IS HARD TO DEFINE.

BUT WE WOULD TRY TO CHANGE THE WORLD AS MUCH AS WE COULD, BEFORE AND AFTER OUR CHILD ARRIVED.

BROOKLYN BECKHAM

Photographing animals in the wild was an unforgettable experience. The thought of them suffering, or a future where they don't exist, is unbearable to me.

We all have to fight for wildlife and our planet, and each do all that we can.

HOW YOU CAN HELP

- Avoid places that offer wildlife interactions or shows.
- Pledge not to buy a wild animal as a pet, or products made from wild animal body parts.
- Support local, ethical tours to observe animals safely and responsibly in the wild, where they belong.

With support from World Animal Protection.

Photography by Brooklyn Beckham.

A GLIMPSE

WRITTEN BY
ROBERT KIRKMAN
ART & COLORS BY
CHARLIE ADLARD

Rover Red Charlie

WRITTEN BY
GARTH ENNIS
ART & COLORS BY
CHAEL DiPASCALE
LETTERING BY
JIM CAMPBELL

HELLO.

I'M CHARLIE, AND THESE ARE MY FRIENDS RED AND ROVER.

IT FEELS FUNNY TALKING TO FEEDERS AGAIN. IN MY WORLD, YOU'RE ALL GONE.

SOME TIME BACK, WE WALKED FROM THE BIG SPLASH TO THE BIGGER SPLASH.

WE CLIMBED THE BIG BIG AND CROSSED THE BIG EMPTY. WE WERE BOUND FOR THE PLACE WHERE THE SUN LIES DOWN.

HOW'S MY ASS, DUDE?

WE FOUGHT THE HISSPOTS, AND HERMANN THE MONSTER. WE LEARNED TO EAT QUACKERS AND BORK-BORKERS.

WE MET BINGO AND SASHA AND AUDIE AND ALBERT. AND HOBBY, THE SADDEST DOG OF ALL.

NOT NOW, RED.

BUT WE WENT BECAUSE ALL THE FEEDERS HAD GONE. EVERY LAST ONE. IN LESS TIME THAN IT TAKES FOR TWO FEEDINGS.

WE WERE TOLD WE COULD FIND MORE FEEDERS. BUT WHEN WE GOT TO THE BIGGER SPLASH, THERE WERE NONE.

AW, JUST A QUICK SNIFF FOR YOUR OLD PAL.

WHAT WE DIDN'T EXPECT... WAS THAT EVER SINCE THEN... IN A WORLD WITHOUT FEEDERS...

WE'VE DONE JUST FINE.

≶HFF≶

≶HFF≶

ALL GOOD, RED.

BUT IF *YOU* FEEDERS DON'T CHANGE YOUR WAYS VERY SOON, YOU'RE GOING TO RUIN YOUR WORLD FOR *EVERYONE.*

OUR WORLD IS A DOG PLACE. YOURS WILL BE NO PLACE.

GET IT?

WHO YOU TALKING TO, CHARLIE?

FEEDERS.

I THOUGHT THEY ALL DISAPPEARED.

YEAH, WELL, THEY'RE WORKING ON IT.

The Future in a Plastic Cup

IT WAS THE EARLY 2000s. I WAS STILL A STUDENT IN PHILADELPHIA. A FEW FRIENDS AND I HAD DECIDED TO GO TO A FOLK FESTIVAL.

IT WAS A THREE-DAY AFFAIR, ON FARM-LAND OUT IN THE MIDDLE OF NOWHERE, CAMPED IN TENTS BY THE BANKS OF A RIVER WHOSE NAME I NOW FORGET.

I REMEMBER PICKING OUT A PLACE, PITCHING A TENT IN THE SCORCHING SUN.

THERE WAS NO ALCOHOL PERMITTED BUT WE SNUCK BOTTLES IN ANYWAY.

OTHER MORE ADVENTUROUS SUBSTANCES COULD BE FOUND IF YOU KNEW THE RIGHT PEOPLE.

WE DANCED AND SANG AND REVELED INTO THE NIGHT UNTIL THE SUN SNUCK UP ON US ONCE AGAIN.

WHEN IT GOT TOO HOT, WE WALKED TO THE NEARBY RIVER, STRIPPED OFF AND DOVE IN.

I REMEMBER THAT WATER--CRISP, FULL OF LAUGHTER AND SUNLIGHT.

ON ONE OF THE NIGHTS, SAT BY A ROARING CAMPFIRE, I MET A MAN NAMED SMOKE, WHO SOLD TIE-DYE T-SHIRTS AND JEWELRY MADE OF BONE.

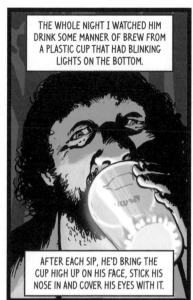

THE WHOLE NIGHT I WATCHED HIM DRINK SOME MANNER OF BREW FROM A PLASTIC CUP THAT HAD BLINKING LIGHTS ON THE BOTTOM.

AFTER EACH SIP, HE'D BRING THE CUP HIGH UP ON HIS FACE, STICK HIS NOSE IN AND COVER HIS EYES WITH IT.

WHAT'S IN THE CUP, SMOKE? I ASKED HIM.

THE FUTURE, MAAAAAN. HE SAID.

WE ALL LAUGHED.

LATER, AS WE WERE LEAVING THE FARM TO GO BACK HOME, I FOUND THE CUP ON THE GROUND, ABANDONED.

NEW YEAR'S EVE, 2012.

NO DOUBT THE PREVIOUS GENERATIONS LEFT US IN A HOLE.

NEW YEAR'S EVE, 2022.

NO SENSE WASTING ANY ENERGY ON WHO'S TO BLAME. IT'S OUR INHERITANCE.

NEW YEAR'S EVE, 2032.

IT'S EASY TO FEEL HOPELESS.

NEW YEAR'S EVE, 2042.

...THAT'S BECAUSE THINGS *LOOK* HOPELESS.

SOON TO BE AN EXCITING APARTMENT COMPLEX

NO GRASS

THE WHOLE WORLD WILL BE CONCRETED OVER, AND WE'LL *SUFFOCATE.*

THEY DON'T UNDERSTAND, YOU SEE.

WE *NEED* THESE PARKS, THESE OPEN SPACES MORE THAN MONEY MADE FROM NEW HOUSES.

IT'S A DISGRACE. THEY'RE NOTHING BUT *ANIMALS.*

THE OLD LADY'S RIGHT. THERE'S NO CONNECTION WITH NATURE ANYMORE. PEOPLE STARE AT *GLOWING SCREENS* RATHER THAN *SUNSETS.*

COME ON, LOVE. NO BEGGING HERE. MOVE ON.

METROPOLITAN POLICE

MOVE WHERE? THEY *EVICTED* ME FROM MY HOUSE!

I'VE GOT *NOWHERE!*

BUT SUNSETS LEAD TO *DARKNESS.*

AND THE DARKNESS IS *COLD,* WHEN YOU'RE LEFT *OUTSIDE.*

I SAID *GET OFF ME!*

WE JUST CONSTRICT IN PLACE, STRUGGLING TO BREATHE AS THE CITIES *CLOSE IN* AROUND US--

--UNTIL WE *BREAK.*

CLATTER

THE STREET GOES *SILENT.* YOUNG AND OLD, RICH AND POOR, FED AND STARVING-- THE GULFS BETWEEN ARE *TOO WIDE* FOR THEM.

THINGS WILL GET *WORSE* BEFORE THEY GET BETTER. PEOPLE NEED TO HAVE A COLLECTIVE MOMENT OF *UNITY,* TO REMEMBER THAT THEY WERE ONCE A *TRIBE--*

--AND SO I *REVEAL* MYSELF.

VERMIN. MANGE-RIDDLED SCAVENGERS. SHOULD BE EXTERMINATED. WE'VE HEARD THEM ALL.

BUT THROUGH ALL OF THIS, WE *SURVIVE.* WE FIND THE SMALL PATCHES OF NATURE IN YOUR CONCRETE PRISONS AND *LIVE.*

AND WHEN WE ARE SEEN, IT'S *MAGICAL. A GOOD OMEN. A MOMENT TO STOP, AND CONSIDER.*

A MOMENT TO *REGAIN SANITY.*

THERE REALLY *WAS* A FOX! GOOD ON YOU FOR NOT HITTING THE POOR THING!

I'LL SORT YOU A PLACE FOR TONIGHT, OKAY?

WE DON'T SPEAK MUCH, BUT IF WE DID? WE'D TELL YOU TO *STOP* DESTROYING YOUR *GREEN* PLACES.

TO BE THANKFUL FOR WHAT YOU *HAVE,* AND TO HELP THOSE THAT *HAVE NOT.*

NOT SO FANTASTIC, MR. FOX

DEVELOPED WITH	WRITTEN BY	ART BY	LETTERING BY
JUDGE ROB RINDER	TONY LEE	NEIL McCLEMENTS	JIM CAMPBELL

NOT JUST TO KEEP THE AIR FRESHER, BUT TO HELP YOUR *OWN* MENTAL HEALTH.

AND WE'D REMIND YOU THAT YOU ARE A *PACK.* A *TRIBE.*

SO *ACT* LIKE ONE.

LISTEN TO *FOXES.* BECAUSE WE'RE LISTENING TO *YOU.* BUILD MORE GREEN SPACES IN YOUR CONCRETE CITY PRISONS--

--AND WE MIGHT JUST COME *VISIT* YOU MORE.

WRITTEN AND DRAWN BY
POLYP

WRITTEN BY | ART BY | LETTERING BY
ALAN MOORE | MELINDA GEBBIE | BERNARDO BRICE

"Frankly, Trevor, this isn't looking good."

WRITTEN AND DRAWN BY
JOEL PETT

Amends

WRITTEN AND DRAWN BY
THE PERRY BIBLE
FELLOWSHIP

The Talk

URTH-01

WRITTEN AND DRAWN BY
MICHAEL LEE HARRIS

LETTERING BY
FRANK CVETKOVIC

GULA!

GULA!

WHAT IS IT, ACERVUS?! THE COMMS ARE FOR **OFFICIAL** USE ONLY!

THIS IS OFFICIAL! IT'S SO COLD HERE I CAN SEE MY BREATH!

SO?!

"SO"?! YOU'RE IN CHARGE OF ENVIRONMENTAL MAINTENANCE!

OH RIGHT!

Food Storage

LEN'S ANIMAL MAGIC

WRITTEN BY	ART BY	COLORS BY	LETTERING BY
SIR LENNY HENRY	MARK BUCKINGHAM	LEE LOUGHRIDGE	TODD KLEIN

I USED TO WORK AT DUDLEY ZOO WHEN I WAS 14-ISH.

I DID ALL SORTS. WASHED DISHES. MOPPED FLOORS.

THEY EVEN LET ME SERVE SOMETIMES.

THE BOSS TRIED TO MAKE IT LOOK LIKE I WAS THE RIGHT AGE...

SOMETIMES ON MY LUNCH BREAK I'D HAVE A QUICK STROLL ROUND THE ZOO. I LOVED LOOKING AT ALL THE ANIMALS...

THE HYENAS WERE PROBABLY MY FIRST AUDIENCE.

MY WIFE'S A RED HEAD.

NO HAIR, JUST A RED HEAD.

MY DOG CAN TALK.

I SAID: HOW'D YOU FEEL THIS MORNING?

HE SAID: RUF.

I WAS ALWAYS THINKING OF THINGS LIKE THAT WHEN I WASN'T WORKING.

I GUESS THAT'S WHERE ALL THE STUPID STUFF COMES FROM.

DUCKS USED TO SCARE ME.

THE DRAKES WERE ALWAYS VERY ROUGH ON THE MALLARDS-- LITERALLY CHASE, CHASE, CHASE-- AND THEN BITE THE NECK AND HAVE THEIR WAY WITH THEM IN BROAD DAYLIGHT.

I ALWAYS THOUGHT IT WAS UNJUST.

MADE ME WANT TO GO INTO...

...DUCK LAW.

YOUR HONOUR, THE *CCTV* CAMERA TELLS US THIS REPREHENSIBLE MALLARD TOOK THIS DUCK BY FORCE. NO DINNER, NO MOVIE, NO NOTHING.

YOUR HONOR, I OBJECT! THAT COULD HAVE BEEN ANY DUCK DOING WHAT HE DID AND SHE KNOWS IT.

THIS FOOTAGE IS THE TRUTH OF WHAT HAPPENED THAT DAY.

THE TRUTH? YOU CAN'T *HANDLE* THE TRUTH!

I ALWAYS THOUGHT CUDDLES THE KILLER WHALE NEEDED A BIGGER POOL. AT LEAST THREE FOOTBALL PITCHES' WORTH. I THINK HE WAS CONSTRAINED BY HIS SURROUNDINGS.

AT LEAST THAT'S WHAT IT FELT LIKE TO ME.

I USED TO GO TO THE DISCO AT THE TOP OF DUDLEY ZOO. THE QUEEN MARY BALLROOM.

YOU HAD TO WALK PAST THE ELEPHANT ENCLOSURE TO GET THERE.

I ALWAYS THOUGHT IT WAS WEIRD FOR THE ELEPHANTS WATCHING US GO IN AND THEN SEEING US COME OUT LATER THAT NIGHT, IN A RIGHT STATE.

I WONDER WHAT THEY THOUGHT OF US?

EVERY WEEK WE SEE THIS. THEY ENTER SMARTLY CLOTHED, CLEAN, SMELLING FRESH.

NO TROUBLE AT ALL.

I KNOW.

AND THEN THEY COME OUT OF THAT PLACE. DRUNK.

FIGHTING LIKE DOGS.

ROLLING AROUND IN THE BUSHES, FORNICATING.

AND WE'RE THE ONES THEY BLOODY LOCK UP.

HAPPY DAYS THOUGH. NOT SURE THE ANIMALS FELT THE SAME WAY. BUT FOR ME? THEY WERE HAPPY DAYS...

END

WRITTEN BY
SCOTT "BABYDADDY" HOFFMAN

ART BY
JUAN BOBILLO

LETTERING BY
BERNARDO BRICE

HE IS FOURTEEN WHEN HE CLIMBS THE THOUSAND BUND.

HE HAD LISTENED THE NIGHT BEFORE, HEARD THE SOUND OF THE GIANT TIDES RECEDING, THEIR FETID STENCH MUTED, AND DECIDED IT WAS TIME.

WRITTEN BY
CHRIS PACKHAM
ART BY
PETER DOHERTY
GLENN FABRY
KAREN HOLLOWAY
ANDREW SAWYERS
CONOR BOYLE
JOHN CHARLES
LETTERING BY
BERNARDO BRICE

HE IS TIRED OF LIVING IN THE SHADOWS, BENEATH THE GIANT WALL THAT KEEPS THE MASSIVE SEAS AT BAY--

--TIRED OF SCRAPING A MISERABLE EXISTENCE AMONG THE RUINS OF WHAT USED TO BE.

THERE'S A WIDE WORLD OUT THERE--CREATURES THE LIKE OF WHICH THEY CAN ONLY DREAM NOW.

HE'S SEEN THEM. SEEN THEM ON THE SKIN OF THE **LIBRARY OF LIFE.**

SHE'D READ BOOKS, SEEN PICTURES. SHE WAS A LIVING RECORD.

WHEN I DIE THEY'RE GOIN' TO **SKIN** ME, BOY, HANG IT UP FOR SHOW.

ONCE HE'D SEEN A BURD, JUST LIKE ONE ON THE LIBRARY OF LIFE. OR THOUGHT HE HAD --

BURD!

BITTA OLD PLASTI.

THINGS AREN'T LIKE THEY USED TO BE.

YOU DREAMERS GET THAT THOUGHT OUT OF YOUR DAMN HEADS! THE BURDS ARE GONE! IT'S ALL GONE!

YEARS BEFORE, NOT LONG AFTER HIS FATHER AND BRUD DIED IN THE THIRD FAMINE, HIS MOTHER TOOK HIM TO SEE THE TREE.

THE LINE OF PILGRIMS WAS SO LONG--THEY'D TURNED BACK WITH JUST A *GLIMPSE* OF ITS SAD, TWISTED SILHOUETTE.

THE WORLD'S *LAST* TREE, THEY SAID.

BUT *THEY* DIDN'T KNOW EVERYTHING.

THERE WERE WONDROUS THINGS OUT THERE, BEYOND THE BUND, THINGS THEY'D HEARD RUMORS OF--GLOWING NEON CITIES, WHERE THE LUCK-BORN LIVED.

AND BEYOND THEM...WHAT? MORE. THERE MUST BE MORE.

IT CAN'T ALL BE DEAD AND TWISTED AND ROTTING AWAY...

WHAT YOU DOIN'?

EHHH...?

FISHING. THAT'S WHAT I'M DOIN'. I'M THE FISHERING MAN.

FISH--IS THAT LIKE A WHALE?

WHAT DO YOU KNOW ABOUT WHALES?

I SEEN 'EM. ON THE LIBRARY OF LIFE. SHE GOT ALL SORTS ON HER, THINGS THAT USED TO BE.

WELL, THERE'S NO WHALES. THERE'S NO FISH. WE KILLED 'EM ALL.

US?

PEOPLE.

SO WHY'RE YOU FISHERIN'?

COS WE GOTTA KEEP TRYIN'. KEEP LOOKIN'. YOU GOTTA HAVE *HOPE*, BOY.

SO I KEEP TRYIN', AND THAT'S ALL I CATCH. CARBAGE. NOTHIN' ELSE LEFT.

THERE'S RATS.

YEAH, THERE'S RATS. AN' BUGS. AN' US. RATS AN' BUGS AN' US.

DON'T KNOW WHICH IS THE BIGGEST PEST.

'LEAST YOU CAN *EAT* RATS AN' BUGS. GUESS THAT MAKES IT US.

NOW CLEAR OFF, BOY. GOT A FISH TO CATCH.

HE CLIMBS THE THOUSAND BUND OFTEN AFTER THAT, AND ALWAYS THE FISHERING MAN IS THERE.

UNTIL ONE DAY HE'S NOT.

'COURSE THEY'LL ALL BE GONE SOON ENOUGH. IF THE NEXT FAMINE DOESN'T GET THEM, THE NEXT PLAGUE WILL.

NOBODY LIVES LONG ANYMORE. THEIR TEETH ROT AND THEIR SKIN FLAKES OFF AND THEIR NAILS FALL OFF. POISONED, LIKE THE LAND.

WHAT HAPPENED TO HIM?

I DON'T KNOW. BIG WAVE MAYBE. SWEPT AWAY.

YOU GOING TO COME BACK?

IF I GET TIME. GONNA BE BUSY. YOU KNOW WHERE I'LL BE.

SO CLIMB THAT THOUSAND BUND, AND THAT'S WHERE YOU'LL SEE HIM--

ANY TIME OF DAY, ALL KINDS OF WEATHER, HE'LL BE THERE, THE FISHERING MAN.

BECAUSE SOMEBODY'S GOT TO DO IT. **SOMEBODY'S** GOT TO KEEP HOPE ALIVE.

FISH?!

SINCE I WAS A CHILD I WAS FASCINATED BY NATURE.

I'D DEVOUR NATURE DOCUMENTARIES WITH MY BROTHER, SITTING THERE AND DREAMING OF SEEING THOSE PLACES FOR MYSELF.

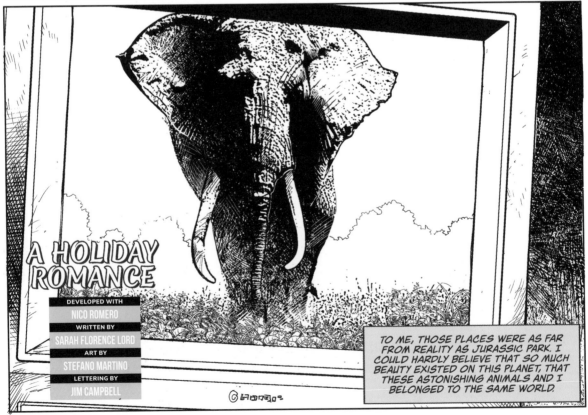

A HOLIDAY ROMANCE

DEVELOPED WITH
NICO ROMERO
WRITTEN BY
SARAH FLORENCE LORD
ART BY
STEFANO MARTINO
LETTERING BY
JIM CAMPBELL

TO ME, THOSE PLACES WERE AS FAR FROM REALITY AS JURASSIC PARK. I COULD HARDLY BELIEVE THAT SO MUCH BEAUTY EXISTED ON THIS PLANET, THAT THESE ASTONISHING ANIMALS AND I BELONGED TO THE SAME WORLD.

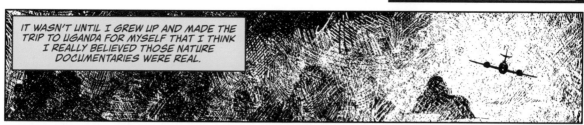

IT WASN'T UNTIL I GREW UP AND MADE THE TRIP TO UGANDA FOR MYSELF THAT I THINK I REALLY BELIEVED THOSE NATURE DOCUMENTARIES WERE REAL.

IT WAS SO DIFFERENT FROM THE WORLD I WAS USED TO, BUT I HAD NEVER FELT MORE MYSELF, MORE AT HOME...

I SAW THINGS THAT MADE ME LAUGH...

...FRIGHTENED ME...

...AND MADE ME CRY. WATCHING THE GORILLAS IS SOMETHING I'LL NEVER FORGET. TO ME IT WAS NATURE IN ITS PUREST FORM.

BEFORE I LEFT SPAIN, I WAS ANXIOUS ABOUT LEAVING BEHIND EVERYTHING THAT CONNECTED ME TO MY REALITY. BUT THAT WAS BEFORE I REALIZED THIS WAS MY REALITY, AND THOSE DISCOMFORTS WERE ACTUALLY FREEDOMS.

BUT EVERY ADVENTURE HAS TO COME TO AN END.

WE ALL HAVE TO COME BACK TO REALITY EVENTUALLY.

BUT IT DOES MAKE YOU WONDER...

DOES IT REALLY HAVE TO BE THAT WAY?

"COME." AND ANOTHER, A **RED HORSE**, WENT OUT;

AND TO HIM WHO SAT ON IT, WAS GRANTED TO TAKE **PEACE** FROM THE EARTH,

AND A GREAT **SWORD** WAS GIVEN TO HIM.

SAVE THE THINGS YOU *LOVE!*

WITH THANKS

STORY CREDITS

INDEX OF CONTRIBUTORS

INDEX OF CONTRIBUTORS...CONT

ACKNOWLEDGMENTS

Works referenced:
p.54 Jean-Jacques Rousseau, non-fiction book, Discourse on Inequality
p.90 Kathy Ketñil-Kijiner, poem, Midnight
p.102 Wangari Maathai, speech at Goldman Awards, 24 April 2006
pp.110-111 Professor Michael E.Mann, non-fiction book, The New Climate War, copyright © 2001. Reprinted by permission of PublicAffairs., an imprint of Hachette Book Group, Inc.
p.145 Sir Nicholas Stern, opinion piece, "The View" in "The South China Morning Post"
p.152 Sir Andrew Lloyd Webber and Sir Trevor Nunn, song, "Memory" from "Cats"
p.183 George Adamson, autobiography, My Pride and Joy
p.185 Eric Bazilian, song, One of Us. Used by Permission / All Rights Reserved
p.267 George Monbiot, non-fiction book, Feral
pp.269-271 Yoko Ono, song, I Love You, Earth. Copyright © Yoko Ono 1985 Used by Permission/ All Rights Reserved. Also, Letters to the Earth campaign
p.272 Marian Greaves, letter, Use Your Voice. Letters to the Earth campaign, which invites letters to be written worldwide in response to the planetary crisis. www.letterstotheearth.com

Photography credits:
The publisher would like to thank the following for their kind permission to reproduce their photographs:
Key: a-above; b-below/bottom; c-center; f-far; l-left; r-right; t-top

Greenpeace: © Greenpeace 6tr, Oscar Siagian / Greenpeace 112-113tr, Paul Hilton / Greenpeace 112bl, Egidio Trainito / Greenpeace 112br, Claudia Carrillo / Greenpeace 113bc
Born Free: ©Daily Mail 6tr, © alwynphoto.com 188-189tr, © Robin Claydon 188bl, © georgelogan.co.uk 188bc, © Sangha Pangolin Project/Maja Gudehus 188br, © BFF 189bc
World Land Trust: Callie Broaddus 6br, Robin Moore 204-205tr, Jo Dale 204bl, FUNDAECO 204br, Dan Bradbury / World Land Trust 205bc
Re:wild: Robin Moore / Re:wild 214-215tr, Aussie Ark 214bl, William Robichaud 214bc, Tilo Nadler 214br, David Stowe / Aussie Ark 215bc
Reserva: The Youth Land Trust: Highland Yearbook Staff 6cr, Callie Broaddus 218-219tr, Callie Broaddus 218bl, Sean Graesser 218bc, Callie Broaddus 218br, Callie Broaddus 219bc
Rewilding Europe: Robin Moore 6ctl, Sandra Bartocha / Wild Wonders of Europe 230-231tr,
Staffan Widstrand / Rewilding Europe 230bl, Magnus Elancer / Wild Wonders of Europe 230bc, Mark Hamblin / Wild Wonders of Europe 230br, Fabrizio Cordischi / Rewilding Apennines 231bc
The Wildlife Trusts: Neil Aldridge 248-249tr, Malcolm Brown 248bl, David Parkyn 248bc, Andy Rouse / 2020VISION 248br, Neil Aldridge 249bc
Stop Ecocide International: Ruth Davey look-again.org 6cbl
Callie Broaddus 7c, 8c, 9c
Dreamstime.com: André Costa 84-85
Native Daily Network 99t
Liberia Chimpanzee Rescue & Protection 173br
Brooklyn Beckham 294t, 294bl, 294br

Additional thanks:
p.6 with thanks to Hector Trunnec for artwork
pp.254-257 A Fevered Mind and a Pot of Pee: An image has been designed using resources from Freepik.com

DK would also like to thank Mark Penfound, Anne Damerell, Jessica DeFerry, Lottie Chesterman, Martin Way, Lisa Moore, Nicola Torode, and Tom Morse for their assistance on this title.

Editorial Beth Davies, Nicole Reynolds
Design James McKeag, Jennifer Murray
Senior Production Editor Jennifer Murray
Senior Production Controller Lloyd Robertson
Managing Editors Pete Jorgensen, Paula Regan
Managing Art Editor Jo Connor
Publishing Director Mark Searle

First published in Great Britain in 2021 by
Dorling Kindersley Limited
DK, One Embassy Gardens, 8 Viaduct Gardens,
London SW11 7BW

The authorised representative in the EEA is
Dorling Kindersley Verlag GmbH. Arnulfstr. 124,
80636 Munich, Germany

10 9 8 7 6 5 4 3 2 1
001–324740–Nov/2021

A CIP catalogue record for this book
is available from the British Library.
ISBN 978-0-24151-351-4

Printed and bound in China

For the curious
www.dk.com

This book has been produced using Forest Stewardship Council™ (FSC) certified materials.
FSC is the gold standard in certification schemes promoting responsible forest management and
protecting the rights of indigenous populations. The inks have been manufactured using vegetable
oils (rather than mineral oil). The cover is finished with a water-based varnish rather than a plastic
laminate. Our print manufacturer is ISO 14001 accredited–this is an international standard for
environmental management ensuring they are measuring their environmental impact and continually
improving their performance year on year.